THE
AUSTRIAN
ACHIEVEMENT
1700–1800

THE
AUSTRIAN
ACHIEVEMENT

1700–1800

ERNST WANGERMANN

with 117 illustrations, 15 in colour

THAMES AND HUDSON · LONDON

For María Josefa

Frontispiece. The ceiling fresco in
the main room of the National
Library (formerly the Imperial
Library), Vienna, painted by
Daniel Gran between 1726 and
1730.

© 1973 THAMES AND HUDSON LTD, LONDON

Printed in Great Britain by Jarrold and Sons Ltd, Norwich

ISBN 0 500 32027 6 *clothbound*
ISBN 0 500 33027 1 *paperbound*

CONTENTS

2 'Summer'. Detail of the ceiling fresco
by Paul Troger in the great hall
of the Abbey of Altenburg. ▶

I should like to express my gratitude to the officials of the State Archives in Vienna, who have complied with my numerous requests with unfailing courtesy. I am indebted to my sister, Mrs G. Ernest, who has looked through the papers of Sir Robert Murray Keith in the British Museum and made transcripts of all passages relevant to the theme of this book.

My work was greatly facilitated by the fact that I was able to consult a large proportion of the printed primary sources in the Brotherton Library of Leeds University. For this I am indebted to Dr E. Langstadt, whose work and ingenuity have secured for the Brotherton Library one of the finest collections of printed sources for eighteenth-century German and Austrian history existing in this country.

E.W.

3 View of a part of Vienna during the Turkish siege of 1683, showing the Turkish siege-trenches, which sometimes cut across attractive suburban gardens.

The title originally suggested for this book was *The Habsburg Achievement*. Ultimately, however, I decided on *The Austrian Achievement*. For it seems to me that the achievements which give the eighteenth-century Habsburg monarchy a claim to be represented in a 'Library of European Civilization' were not exclusively, or even primarily, Habsburg achievements.

The initiatives which eventually produced the achievements were, of course, Habsburg initiatives. In a near-absolute monarchy it could hardly have been otherwise. The determined resistance offered by the Austrian Habsburgs in the seventeenth century to the attempt to establish a Bourbon hegemony in Europe is, therefore, the starting-point of our story. The struggle against Bourbon hegemony culminated at the end of the century in the Austrian Habsburgs' assertion of a claim to the inheritance of the defunct Spanish line.

Habsburg successes against France owed a great deal to the support of the maritime powers, England and the United Provinces, which was more or less assured after 1689. But it is truly astonishing that during the short intervals in this long-drawn-out struggle, the Habsburg armies, supported by the Holy Roman Empire, Poland and Venice, were able to parry a mighty Turkish offensive, and soon after to expel the Turks in headlong rout from eastern Hungary. The daring vigour and military genius of Eugene of Savoy were the decisive factors here. Having been refused a regiment by Louis XIV, because of his doubtful reputation at the French court, he entered the service of the Emperor Leopold I when Habsburg fortunes were at their lowest ebb, and triumphed over the Turks in a series of spectacular campaigns between 1683 and 1718. He also contributed substantially to the frustration of Louis XIV's effort to

4 Prince Eugene's bed in the Kaiserzimmer, Abbey of St Florian.

7 Eugene of Savoy. ▶

5 Statue of Leopold I from the Pestsäule in Vienna. Representation in a kneeling position is characteristic of Leopold.

gain the entire Spanish inheritance for the Bourbons by expelling the Bourbon armies from Italy and joining Marlborough in the conquest of the Spanish Netherlands. Altogether, the Habsburgs were doing so well that by 1711, when the death of the Emperor Joseph I made his brother Charles heir to, or claimant of, both the Spanish and the Austrian Habsburg inheritance, it was possible to fear that a Habsburg rather than a Bourbon hegemony was threatening Europe.

This fear was one of the factors in Britain's defection from the Grand Alliance in 1712, which put Spain and its American colonies out of the Emperor Charles VI's reach. Despite this

◀ 6 Ivory statuette of Charles VI.

cruel dimming of glorious perspectives, the Habsburg monarchy, formerly little more than a central European satellite of Spain, now claimed recognition as a 'great power' in its own right. In the east, it gained far more than its allies did from the Turkish débâcle. Above all, Hungary was reconquered, and accepted the Habsburgs as hereditary kings. In the west, it entered upon the Spanish inheritance in Italy and the Netherlands. Clearly, the Habsburg monarchy had emerged as a great power.

But had it? There are good grounds for expressing some doubts on the point. Though on the map the Habsburg monarchy after 1718 might seem the equal of France and the supreme power within the Holy Roman Empire, Habsburg power was in reality much inferior to that of France, while Brandenburg-Prussia would shortly reveal that a state of dual supremacy was coming into existence in the Empire. For territorial extent was never in itself the decisive factor in power. Far more important were homogeneity, compactness, a regular revenue from taxation and facilities for profitable commercial enterprise. With all these, the Habsburg monarchy, for all its impressive new acquisitions, was distinctly under-endowed.

Italy and the Netherlands had been restive under Spanish rule. A new Austrian administration, encouraging the participation of the indigenous people, might have been successful and yielded the ruling power dividends in terms of influence and strength. But Charles VI insisted on ruling these countries as 'King of Spain', a title he did not formally renounce till 1726, and used them as pasture for his numerous retinue of exiled Spanish followers, mainly Catalans. Their administration made Austrian rule universally unpopular in Italy and the Netherlands, and paved the way for the later military disasters in these countries.

It is very doubtful whether the acquisition of lands so distant from Vienna as Sicily, Belgium and Serbia represented any increase in Habsburg power at all. It is more likely that the need to provide for their defence resulted in a net drain on Habsburg resources. Prince Eugene, who had played the leading role in

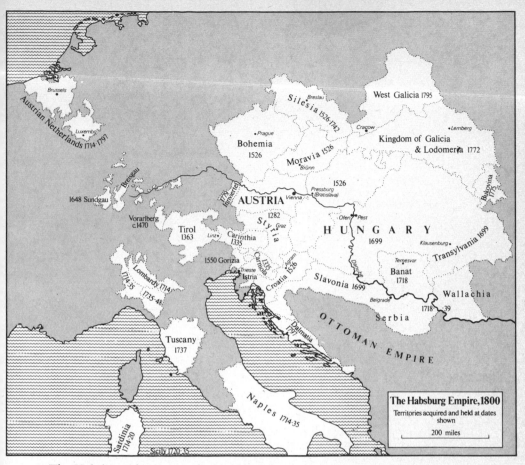

8 The Habsburg dominions during the eighteenth century.

the conquest of these lands, had no illusions on this point. He
believed that only the acquisition of an adjacent territory like
Bavaria would bring the power required to ensure the defence
of the earlier acquisitions. He therefore advised Charles to seek
a Bavarian marriage for his eldest daughter Maria Theresa.
The acquisition of Bavaria, however, though repeatedly
attempted, remained a prize beyond the reach of eighteenth-
century Habsburg statecraft.

13

In the Middle Ages, power depended on the number of followers who could be raised in time of war. In the nineteenth century, it increasingly depended on the productive capacity of a country's basic industries. In the early eighteenth century, it depended above all on the size of a country's permanent military establishment. On the basis of his regular revenues, Charles VI could maintain a permanent military establishment roughly half the size of that of France, and only slightly larger than that of Brandenburg-Prussia. He could maintain a greater force only with the aid of foreign subsidies. This state of affairs could be improved only by an increase in regular revenue from taxation, which in turn could not be achieved except on the basis of far-reaching political and economic reform. Without such reform, the recent territorial acquisitions of the Habsburg monarchy represented a drain on resources rather than an accretion of power, and would always be a temptation to aggressive and powerful neighbours. Their security alone required an internal transformation of the monarchy. As Prince Eugene put it, the monarchy must become 'a whole'. In other words, if the Habsburg monarchy was to survive as it had evolved by 1718, it was necessary to create 'Austria'. But this was not achieved during the reign of Charles VI.

The assertion that the Habsburg monarchy had emerged as a great power by the early eighteenth century therefore requires substantial qualification. If it was widely believed at the time, this was because it was easy to be deceived by superficial phenomena. At the time, it was as easy to underestimate the power of Brandenburg-Prussia, whose ruler Frederick William I affected a harsh, bourgeois–Calvinist modesty, as it was to over-estimate that of the Habsburg monarchy, whose ruler Charles VI seized every opportunity of outwardly manifesting his dignities and claims, not only as head of the House of Austria, but as German Emperor and King of Spain as well. Though we are not so deceived today, the monarchy of Charles VI may legitimately lay claim to our attention. It may do so because of the manner in which the dignities and powers of Charles VI, so

9 The Karlskirche, Vienna, designed by J. B. Fischer von Erlach and completed by his son in 1737.

problematical in reality, were given symbolic representation in the language of art and architecture. While Prince Eugene's triumphs had not won the Habsburg monarchy secure great power status, they had created the conditions for a unique flowering of the creative arts. Though Charles VI failed to make good his claim to Spain, the twin columns, the pillars of Hercules, symbolizing this claim, make the Karlskirche in Vienna, which he commissioned, one of the most original and monumental Baroque churches in Europe.

Sooner or later, inevitably, reality caught up with symbolic representation, and the more grandiose architectural projects of Charles's reign remained unfinished. Before the end of the reign, the Habsburg monarchy was involved in a struggle not

10 J. B. Fischer von Erlach's triumphal arch for the marriage of the Archduke Joseph, later Emperor Joseph I, in 1699. The acceptance of Fischer's designs for Joseph's triumphal arches marked the beginning of the end of the Italian monopoly of architectural commissions.

11 J. B. Fischer von Erlach's first project for the Imperial palace of Schönbrunn. The main building was to be erected on the summit of the hill, to maximize the symbolic grandeur of the structure.

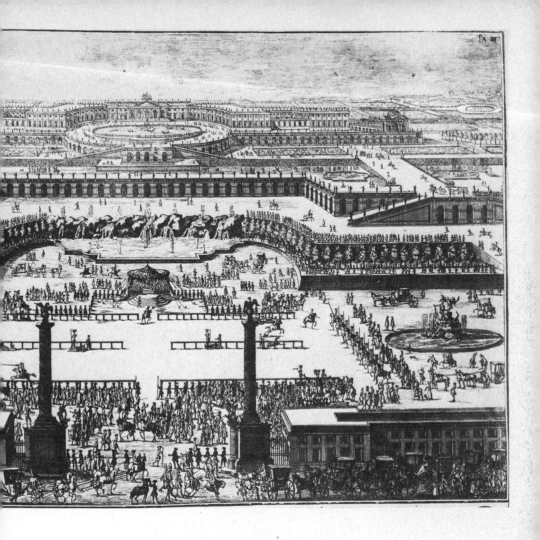

for hegemony, but for survival. Quite early in this struggle, the underlying weaknesses of the monarchy were revealed, and some important territories were lost for good – the Kingdom of Naples (1738), Serbia with the fortress of Belgrade (1739), and the Duchy of Silesia, a valuable part of the original Habsburg possessions (1742). Through this struggle for survival, the Habsburg monarchy became significant for European history in a new way. For, as a result of it, Charles's successors, his daughter Maria Theresa and her son Joseph, were impelled to undertake that transformation of the monarchy into 'a whole' which statesmen like Prince Eugene had long ago recognized as the essential condition for its survival, and which profoundly affected the interests of the most powerful social and political groups.

The reforms, like everything else, sprang from a Habsburg initiative. But they were far more than a Habsburg achievement. The Habsburg system of government, like the Bourbon, but unlike the Hohenzollern, gave plenty of scope to ministerial criticism and initiative. After the earliest reforms, which were carried out in the face of the hostility or indifference of the senior Ministers, ministerial co-operation and initiative became an increasingly important factor. With the establishment of the Council of State in 1761, it becomes virtually impossible to distinguish between the initiatives of the Empress (or of her husband and son) and that of her councillors. Of growing importance, too, was the role played by men in the middle or lower ranks of the new bureaucracy through whom the influence of the Enlightenment was beginning to be brought to bear upon Habsburg government. But for their enthusiasm, which was thrown into the scales against the powerful influence of the ruling classes, the Habsburg achievement would have been much more modest than it was. Some of them urged more radical changes than either Maria Theresa or Joseph II were prepared to entertain.

Nevertheless, the legislation initiated and implemented by Maria Theresa and Joseph, and largely maintained by Joseph's younger brother Leopold in the face of formidable opposition from the nobility and clergy, was more substantial than any previously attempted in a single historical period, and represents, I think, the climax of reforming absolutism in Europe.

The increase in military power, for the sake of which the reforms were undertaken in the first place, was to some extent

achieved. Without it, the Habsburg monarchy could not have

played the role it did in the struggle against Napoleonic domination. But more significant from the point of view of European civilization were the accompanying political, social and cultural changes. A measure of unity and cohesion was imposed on the diverse territories. 'Austria' was created – a political and cultural community with a richly diverse ethnic basis. Moreover, the process of unification involved the re-establishment of contact with the mainstream of European civilization from which the militant Counter-Reformation had virtually isolated the Habsburg monarchy in the seventeenth century. This contact produced some consequences which had been neither foreseen nor intended. The new Austria soon generated a ferment of popular political involvement, comment and criticism which was unparalleled in the rest of the German-speaking world. And at another level the most advanced moral and political ideas of the later eighteenth century found a unique expression in the music of the great Austrian composers of the time. Thus, while Austria gained for herself only a modest place among the great powers, she made one of the most important contributions to European civilization.

In the following pages, the term 'Austrian' is not used in a narrow, ethnic sense, but to refer to that new political and cultural sense of community, transcending ethnic divisions, which emerged within the Habsburg monarchy during the eighteenth century. Partly because the Habsburg rulers continued to secure election as German Emperors, the Habsburg monarchy attracted talented men from the Empire throughout the eighteenth century. Jurists seeking state employment, writers sensing the attraction of a metropolis, businessmen responding to governmental incentives – many such men came from outside to establish themselves permanently in the territories ruled by the Habsburgs. They and their achievements are described as 'Austrian' in this book. I believe this to be justified chiefly because they regarded themselves as such, and not as foreign residents. That in itself is not the least of the Austrian achievements in the period under review.

Ihro Käy[serliche] Mayst[ät]: haben auf den Neunzehen,
den April: siebenzehenhundert und drey:
zehen: und Jahren läs[en] allen hero alhier in
Wienn anwesenden Geheimben Räthen an
dem gewöhnlichen ohrt Zu[r]ch seinem ansagen
lassen.   Alß nun die bestimbte Stund
herbey kommen, haben Sich Ihre Käy[serliche] Mayst[ät]
in Ihro Geheimben Raths=Stuben unter
den Baldachin begeben, und Vor den gewöhn=
lichen Räythsch: tisch gestellet, darauf auch Ihro
Geheimbe Räthe und Ministros seinen her=
=unssen, diese jedoch in ihrer ordnung ein=
=getreeten. und Jeder an seinem ohrt
stehend geblieben;   Alß: bists Prinz Eu=
=genius Von Savoyen. fürst Von Trau[t]=
=sohn, fürst Von Schwarzenberg. Graff
Von Traun LandMarschall. Graff Von
Thürn Ihro Käy[serliche] Mayst[ät]: Eleonora Obrist
HoffMaister. Graff Von dietrichstein Obrist
Stallmaister. Graff Von Seilern HoffCant[z]=
=ler. Graff Von Starhenberg Camer=Präsi=
=dent. Graff Von Martiniz Junior.

FINDING A BASIS FOR GREAT POWER STATUS

By a painful irony of fate, the precarious basis of the Habsburg monarchy's great power status was dramatically illustrated by the problem of the succession, which threatened it with division and disintegration on the very morrow of its great triumphs in the Turkish and French Wars. When he signed the Treaty of Rastatt in 1714, the Emperor Charles VI was the last male representative of his line. Not even a daughter had been born to him. The court at Vienna was distraught by problems of precedence, which was hotly disputed among a plethora of dowager empresses and archduchesses, widows and daughters of the lately deceased emperors (Leopold I, 1705, and Joseph I, 1711). More serious, there was talk of dividing the monarchy among them all, and the Hungarians discussed the possibility of their Diet electing a king from another dynasty.

Charles's legal and political advisers countered this threat to the permanence of the monarchy by the solemn proclamation of a new Order of Succession for the House of Austria based on Spanish precedents – the Pragmatic Sanction (1713). It asserted the indivisibility of the entire monarchy and the right of female succession in the absence of a male heir. Charles's daughters, if any, were to have precedence over his late brother's, and these over Leopold's daughters. The government secured formal acceptance of the Pragmatic Sanction by the Estates of all the Austrian and Bohemian lands, its adoption as a law by the Hungarian Diet (1722), and its guarantee by one after the other of the European powers. This was a considerable and worthwhile achievement, though it was not of course in itself a guarantee that Charles's elder daughter Maria Theresa, born in 1717, would succeed to an undivided inheritance.

21

◀ 12 A page from the Pragmatic Sanction, 1713.

The financial resources of the Habsburg monarchy were grossly inadequate for the role which it was beginning to assume in international affairs under Leopold I. More than once Prince Eugene had to go into battle at the head of an unpaid, underfed and ill-equipped army; to lead such an army to victory was indeed one of his more astonishing feats. When the Habsburg government *was* able to supply numerous armies and keep them fighting in distant theatres of war, this was generally due to the credit and resourcefulness of the Vienna 'Court Jews' (*Hofjuden*), above all Samuel Oppenheimer and Samson Wertheimer. After the economic ravages wrought by the militant Counter-Reformation and the Thirty Years War, only

13 'Supreme War Contractor and Court Jew': Samuel Oppenheimer, represented with some of his stock-in-trade.

14 Lottery in the Haus zur Mehlgrube. The municipal lottery provided the city of Vienna with some of its regular income.

the Jewish communities managed to preserve and develop an international network of credit and exchange in central and eastern Europe. In nearly every crisis during the French and Turkish Wars, only the big Jewish bankers were able to provide large amounts of cash when and where required, or willing to furnish military provisions for payment other than cash. Oppenheimer's death and the consequent bankruptcy of his firm in 1703 was, therefore, the cause of a major crisis for the monarchy as a whole.[1] Oppenheimer and Wertheimer, by providing the essential sinews of war, did as much as the generals and statesmen to enable the Habsburg monarchy to play the part of a great power in the early eighteenth century.

After the wars, serious efforts were made to improve the monarchy's finances. The Vienna City Bank, founded in 1705, began to rival the Court Jews in the provision of government

23

loans. The government sponsored and fostered this institution in order that the state might be able to benefit from the credit and the sound financial position of the city of Vienna. The revenues of some royal mines and tolls were made over to the bank, which assumed the obligation of advancing money to the government as and when required. Under the capable direction of Thomas Gundakar Starhemberg, the Vienna City Bank brought some semblance of order to Habsburg finances, at least in peacetime.[2]

The close connection between revenues adequate to sustain great power status and a flourishing national economy was fully appreciated in Habsburg government circles at this time. Already in the 1670s and 1680s a group of talented and enthusiastic publicists of the 'cameralist' school had come from various parts of the Empire to Vienna and had successfully preached mercantilist doctrine. Their writings and projects show us the importance they attached to Dutch and English experience and, in the light of this, their belief in the enormous economic potential of the Habsburg dominions.[3] This conviction finds admirable expression in the title of Philipp Wilhelm Hörnigk's work published in 1684, *Österreich über alles, wenn es nur will.*

The influence of the cameralists can be clearly discerned in the government's attempt to work out and implement a coherent policy of economic growth, an attempt which increasingly influenced Habsburg internal and foreign policy from the 1670s. A basic weakness of this policy was its neglect of agriculture which, in these pre-physiocratic days, was still largely in a state of stagnation as a result of the deadweight of uncontrolled feudal exploitation. The three-field system of crop-raising and extensive pasture remained the rule. The harvest amounted on the average to only three to five times the volume of seed.[4] The only government action in the field of agriculture during these years was the successful colonization of the Temesvár Banat, which was virtually depopulated when it was ceded by Turkey after the Battle of Peterwardein (1717).

15 The Bohemian method of glass-blowing. An illustration from the *Encyclopédie* of Diderot and d'Alembert.

However, a great deal of attention was paid to manufacture and trade, the over-all mercantilist aim being to retain capital inside the state and to stimulate its circulation within it. The government invested state funds directly in factories, for example, a mirror factory at Neuhaus in Lower Austria (1701) and a porcelain factory just outside Vienna (1718). It also encouraged the most substantial private owners of capital – manorial lords, abbeys and trading companies – to do likewise. The modern factory-based textile industry in the Habsburg monarchy was in fact born on some of the great manors of Austria and Bohemia. These new factories employed labour both directly and indirectly by 'putting-out'. The Linz textile factory, owned for a time by the Oriental Company, employed twelve thousand workers by the middle of the eighteenth century.[5]

The output of the Austrian iron industry also increased after prolonged stagnation, and again reached the peak level which it had attained during its heyday in the sixteenth century. The mining of precious metals was profitably carried on despite competition from the New World, and the vigour of this industry is well illustrated by the fact that already in 1723 steam-engines of the type developed by Newcomen were draining water from flooded shafts in the north Hungarian copper-mines. They were installed by Joseph Emanuel Fischer von Erlach, the son of the famous architect Johann Bernhard.[6] If full industrial statistics were available, they would probably show that the most spectacular boom was enjoyed by the building industry as a result of the astonishing building craze which affected nearly all classes of society after the triumph over the Turks. This also owed something to the prevailing mercantilist influence, inasmuch as the government applied moral pressure, and provided material incentives, to encourage building projects, with the aim of bringing 'dead' capital into circulation and stimulating employment.[7]

16 The Palais Trautson, Vienna, designed by J.B. Fischer von Erlach in 1709, shows the influence of contemporary English architecture.

17 The harbour of Trieste in the eighteenth century.

The government's concern with stimulating trade is best illustrated by its determination to lose no time in exploiting the commercial possibilities opened up by the retreat of the Turks. The policy of establishing trade-routes through the newly conquered territories, and markets in the towns still under the control of the defeated enemy, culminated in the comprehensive commercial treaty with the Porte concluded as part of the settlement of Passarowitz (1718). The victorious power insisted no less firmly on the admission of its merchants on favoured terms than on the cession of territories and fortresses.[8]

The bid to secure for the Habsburg monarchy a share of the lucrative Far Eastern trade, based on the newly acquired Atlantic ports of the Netherlands, was foiled by the jealousy and determined hostility of Britain and the United Provinces: it was given up in return for these countries' guarantee of the Pragmatic Sanction. In the Adriatic, on the other hand, Austria was more successful. The fact that she profited more from the triumph over the Turks than her allies did is shown above all by her ensuing success in breaking the centuries-old Venetian monopoly of the Adriatic trade. Even if the proclamation of freedom of trade in the Adriatic (1717) was initially no more than a declaration of intent,[9] Austria's free ports in the Adriatic, above all Trieste and Rijeka (Fiume), attracted a steadily increasing number of ships, including Venetian ships. By the middle of the century, eighty to a hundred different types of commodities were passing through these ports. The Austrian government kept the promise which it had made when the ports were declared free in 1719, that the access routes would be improved. Wide roads were built over the Semmering and the Loibl passes, and they removed the most formidable of the obstacles between the main Austrian manufacturing centres and the Adriatic outlets. When in the 1730s the traditional overland routes of Austrian commerce to the Baltic and North Sea ports were obstructed by new tolls (an early incident in the nascent Austro-Prussian rivalry within the Empire), it was already possible to divert the bulk of the goods affected along the improved routes to the Adriatic.[10]

Nevertheless, the achievements of Habsburg commercial policy were far from matching the potentialities glimpsed by the cameralists. We shall examine below the factors which hindered the full realization of these potentialities. Even so, by the middle of the eighteenth century the Habsburg monarchy was cutting a respectable figure in the Mediterranean and Levant trade, and had at least made a promising start with the task of securing an adequate economic basis for its great power status.

THE SYMBOLS OF POWER AND GREATNESS
The manner in which the Habsburg monarchy's claim to great power status found outward expression in buildings and related works of art has always aroused wonder and admiration. Austrian architecture, painting and sculpture of this period undoubtedly reached and maintained an astonishingly high level of sustained inspiration. After a century or more in which

most creative work in these fields was monopolized by Italians, Austria produced two generations of artists of genius who felt and expressed the self-confidence, pride and sheer joy of life called forth by the country's political and economic progress.

Though there can, perhaps, be no 'historical explanation' for such a phenomenon, it is within the historian's competence to try to explain the nature of the commissions (that is, the nature of the challenge to which the artists had to respond), and to try to identify the ideas and influences which helped to determine the manner in which the commissions were translated into visual forms.

Underlying the court commissions (those from the great noble families and abbeys will be discussed below) is the fact that the Habsburg rulers of this period represented a multiple dignity. They were not only the heads of the House of Austria, celebrating signal triumphs over their hereditary enemies. They were also Roman Emperors and German Kings, the first sovereigns in Europe, defending and reasserting their primacy against the challenge of the Roi Soleil. And for many years after the Treaties of Utrecht and Rastatt they were also maintaining a solemn and inflexible claim to the Crown of Spain. All this was intended to find, and did find, expression in the great buildings and fresco paintings commissioned by the court. Indeed, as has recently been shown in relation to the new Imperial Library (Hofbibliothek) in Vienna, building, painting and statuary were the precise visual expression of an elaborate 'programme' or allegory, not of the artist's invention, relating to the titles, achievements and functions claimed for the sovereign.[11]

Johann Bernhard Fischer von Erlach's first project for the Imperial summer palace at Schönbrunn (recalling, but at the same time overshadowing, Versailles) was clearly intended to symbolize Habsburg primacy over the upstart Louis XIV. Donato Felice d'Allio's commission to build an Imperial residence abutting on to the Abbey of Klosterneuburg near Vienna represented the desire of the would-be King of Spain

29

18 Detail of an allegory of Charles VI from the frescoes by Gran in the National Library (formerly the Imperial Library), Vienna.

for an Austrian equivalent of the Escorial. The unusual twin columns of Fischer's Karlskirche, and in the Prunksaal of the Imperial Library, represent the pillars of Hercules, and thus also symbolize the claim to the Spanish inheritance. The Library as a whole, now recognized as the work of the elder Fischer von Erlach, was designed to celebrate Charles VI as both victor on the battlefield and patron of the arts: it was the temple of the *Hercules Musarum*.[12]

The nature of these commissions and programmes could not fail to give a distinctive imprint to the resulting creations, setting them apart from the Baroque creations of the earlier generation of Italian builders. This has been noted by art historians, who have been searching for an appropriate term with which to describe this distinctiveness. The term 'Imperial Baroque' (*Kaiserstil*) has been suggested and is still used.[13] While this term is useful to distinguish the work of Fischer von Erlach from the Italian Baroque out of which it developed, it does not take us very much further. It defines the 'programmes' to which Fischer had to work, rather than the distinctive manner in which, as is generally agreed, he put these programmes into the language of form. And it is the latter which is of paramount interest to us today.

30

19 The central hall (*Prunksaal*) of the National Library, designed by J. B. Fischer von Erlach (1722), showing one of the two sets of twin columns representing the Pillars of Hercules and thus the claim to the Spanish Crown. ▶

Fischer had travelled widely and was deeply influenced by what he saw and the people he met. In the 1690s he had been to England and had acquainted himself with the work, perhaps with the person, of Sir Christopher Wren. After his return from England he embarked on a pioneering attempt at a comprehensive history and philosophy of world architecture.[14] He was in communication with Leibniz, some of whose ideas he was capable of understanding, and who proposed him as member of the projected Vienna Academy of Sciences. It has been convincingly suggested that Fischer's acquaintance with Europe outside Austria and Italy, his scholarly knowledge of the great styles of the past, and his Leibnizian *Weltanschauung* were the determining factors underlying his distinctive style. His knowledge of England encouraged him to combine the most 'modern' style of his time, Palladian Classicism, with the traditional Italian Baroque of his teacher Bernini. His acquaintance with the history of architecture prompted him to attempt the integration of an astonishing variety of contrasting styles. His Leibnizian vision of God as the rational and benevolent architect of the best possible world entailed the challenge to enter into 'a kind of partnership' with him to create a palace, a church, a library, which would reflect in their own limited spheres the perfection of the world.[15]

Setting his aims so high, Fischer von Erlach created works whose significance far transcended the apotheosis of Charles VI. If the hypothesis of a relationship to the ideas of Leibniz is valid, it could be said that they heralded the approach of the Enlightenment. In any case, it would be difficult to suggest a term that would adequately define their distinctive character.

OVER-MIGHTY SUBJECTS

A number of the great noble families and abbeys had already begun building on a large scale during the last three decades of the seventeenth century. The urge to build on a large scale derived both from the need for much rebuilding and reconstruction after the widespread devastation wrought by the

Turkish invaders, and from the desire to give concrete expression to the wealth and power with which the consolidation of the 'second feudalism' and a century of militant Counter-Reformation had endowed the landed nobility and the Catholic church. The work of designing and supervising the erection of the new buildings was put into the hands of Italians: the Carlones in Upper Austria; Caratti, Porta and others in Bohemia. These great architects developed the Roman and north Italian styles, and created the massive and impressive splendours of the High Baroque. In monastic architecture the greatest possible contrast became apparent between the austere functionalism of the convents housing the missionary Orders of the Counter-Reformation, and the lavish magnificence now commissioned by ambitious and cultured abbots of the old-established Benedictine, Cistercian and Augustinian houses. The fresco paintings required for the vaulted roofs and domes of the new-style abbey churches, libraries and marble halls were also commissioned from Italian masters of the art. In the 1690s the most celebrated of the Italian fresco painters, Andrea Pozzo, followed a call to Vienna where, among other things, he brought some High Baroque colour and splendour to the hitherto dark and austere Jesuit church. Austrian artists appeared here and there in the role of skilled craftsmen carrying out Italian conceptions and designs. Only a handful of Austrian sculptors, among them Rauchmiller, the Strudel brothers and Steinl, worked alongside the Italians as independent creative artists.

At the turn of the century, the period of the decisive triumph over the Turks, a very significant change took place. Austrian architects and designers emerged from their subordinate position and were increasingly commissioned to take charge of the great building projects. The court helped to set the new fashion by accepting Fischer von Erlach's design for a triumphal arch to mark the return of Archduke Joseph as King of the Romans in 1691, and by giving him an official court appointment. Between that year and the outbreak of the War of the Spanish Succession, Fischer was commissioned by Prince

20 Berthold Dietmayr (1670–1739), Abbot of Melk, who commissioned Austrian artists to undertake the rebuilding, on ambitious lines, of his abbey.

Eugene, Count Althann and other nobles to build both winter and summer palaces, and by the Archbishop of Salzburg to build the university church in that city. The abbeys followed suit when in 1702 Abbot Dietmayr of Melk signed a contract with Jakob Prandtauer, putting him in charge of the projected rebuilding of the great monastery on the Danube. Six years later, on the death of Carlo Carlone, Prandtauer assumed control of the building operations in the great Upper Austrian abbeys of St Florian, Kremsmünster and Garsten. After Prandtauer died in 1726 most of his still unfinished work was completed by his pupil Joseph Munggenast. Meanwhile, Johann Lukas Hildebrandt, born in Italy but not an Italian, was employed by the Imperial Vice-Chancellor Schönborn for nearly all his building projects, and by Eugene for his summer residence, the famous Belvedere. When he was asked to undertake also the

21 Count Gundaker Althann, Charles VI's Director of Buildings, handing
the Emperor an inventory of his picture gallery.

rebuilding of the magnificently situated Abbey of Göttweig, he already had so many tasks in hand that he was unable to complete this ambitious project before the onset of another period of warfare compelled him to abandon it. In Bohemia the Dientzenhofers, a German family of architects who had settled in Prague, replaced the Italians as the foremost church-builders of the province.

At the same time as the Austrian architects were taking over nearly all the major architectural commissions, Austrian painters succeeded in breaking the Italian monopoly of fresco painting. Abbot Dietmayr of Melk must be mentioned again as one of the first patrons to give an Austrian painter the chance to prove himself in this field, when he entrusted Johann Michael Rottmayr from Salzburg with the decoration of the ceiling and dome of the abbey church. Thereafter we find Rottmayr, along with Paul Troger and Daniel Gran in the Austrian provinces and Wenzel Reiner in Bohemia, sharing the most important and challenging commissions with the famous Italian masters of the art.

22 Johann Lukas von Hildebrandt's project for the rebuilding of Göttweig Abbey, commissioned by Abbot Gottfried Bessel. The crisis resulting from the War of the Austrian Succession prevented the completion of this ambitious undertaking.

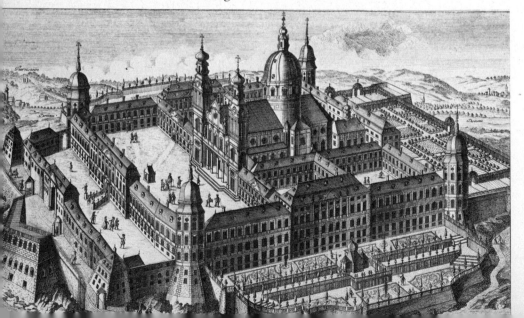

23 The Benedictine Abbey of Melk, rebuilt by Jakob Prandtauer, seen from across the Danube.

24 The Benedictine Abbey of Melk. Ceiling fresco by J.M. Rottmayr (1654–1730).

A remarkable feature of this new generation of artists of the first rank was the prominence of Tiroleans. Prandtauer, Munggenast and Troger were all born in the province of Tirol, with its long tradition of emigration, while Rottmayr was a native of near-by Salzburg. The new generation, though deeply rooted in the Italian tradition – most of them had spent a few years of study with an Italian master in Venice, Rome or Naples – developed a distinctive style. The ponderous and solemn legacy of Roman Baroque receded. The emphasis was on daring innovation of line, and on new decorative elements, in the spirit of Borromini and Guarini. There is a sense of movement which, without detracting from the dignity of the buildings, adds a welcome note of joyful light-heartedness. The sacred buildings no longer enshrine the conscious posture and pathos of Counter-Reformation Baroque. Religious feeling is expressed in simple, human terms, and does not exclude a joyful affirmation of the material world in the building as a whole. Caravaggio, it has been suggested, was the chief inspiration of Troger's paintings, with their intensely human,

25 Staircase in the Schloss Mirabell, Salzburg, by Hildebrandt (1722). ▶

'anti-Baroque' rendering of religious themes.[16] Most important of all is the successful integration of the buildings with the surrounding Austrian countryside. Prandtauer's west façade of Melk, towering over the defile of the Danube as it enters the Wachau, Steinl's and Munggenast's stone spire at Dürnstein, make an unforgettable impression precisely because of this. I know of no places where it would be more difficult to imagine the landscape without the buildings which have been created within it. For all its Italian roots and its continuing Italianate features, the distinctive style of this generation may appropriately be called 'Austrian Baroque'.

All these buildings were in one way or another allegories of the wealth and power of the church and the nobility. That the allegories of wealth were no exaggerations may be seen by casting a glance at the figures relating to the sums spent on buildings. Given a certain degree of competence and economy in the management of the estate, a noble landowner or abbot could evidently make a considerable annual sum available for building operations. It has been calculated that the Abbey of St Florian in Upper Austria could spare up to 12,000 florins and Melk up to 27,000 florins per annum.[17] The greatest noble families, such as the Liechtensteins, could spare even more. That sums of this order could be spent on representation is of course symptomatic of a prospering economy. That they *were* so spent, however, was symptomatic of a very unhealthy distribution of the national income and of political power. It was symptomatic of a social and political order which seriously impeded the full realization of the Habsburg monarchy's economic potential, and thus prevented the development of an adequate basis for its newly acquired status as a great power.

The clergy and nobility, though not in principle exempt from direct taxation (except in Hungary), managed in practice to put themselves into a very lightly taxed category, especially in peacetime.[18] The wealthiest nobles, instead of paying taxes, took to lending the government money for interest. The burden on the peasantry was proportionately excessive. But the peasantry, in addition to bearing an unfair share of the tax burden, was exposed to uncontrolled feudal exploitation. This was particularly exacting in the lands of the Bohemian Crown, where the new aristocracy which had replaced the rebellious Protestants after the Battle of the White Mountain (1620) could treat their estates as conquered land. All the earlier legal rights of the peasants were specifically declared abolished.[19] If the demesne was profitable, the lord could add land to it by abolishing peasant holdings.

In the Austrian provinces, where security of peasant tenure was the rule, the rate of exploitation also increased. Traditional manorial rents and dues rose sharply in the period 1650–1740. If a lord introduced a new crop on the demesne, additional labour services were exacted; but if a crop was abandoned, the services which had been required for its cultivation were not allowed to lapse but commuted to money payments. Peasant indebtedness was common.[20] Here we undoubtedly have the root causes of the low productivity and stagnation of Austrian agriculture.

The property of the church was still growing through new endowments and the 'dowries' which novices from wealthy families brought with them into their chosen foundations. In 1733, there were among the monks of Altenburg in Lower Austria twenty-two of noble descent, three of whom had brought 200,000 florins to the abbey with them, which helped to pay for its reconstruction on an ambitious scale.[21] The wealth of the church had a double significance for the state. Not only was it subject to a relatively light rate of taxation, it was also the basis of the paramount influence which the church exercised over important aspects of internal policy. The church still insisted on a policy of uncompromising confessionalism, and expected the government to suppress the open exercise of Lutheran or any other 'heretical' worship. But this was quite incompatible with the consistent pursuit of mercantilist policies. More important, it prevented Habsburg power from reaping the full benefit of the reconquest of Hungary. This could only

41

have been achieved if it had been possible to extend the semi-absolute form of government, which had evolved in the Austrian and Bohemian provinces, to the reconquered kingdom. But this, in turn, was possible only with the firm support of the Protestant towns and the Hungarian Protestants. Richelieu had been able to lay the foundations of French absolutism only after achieving an understanding with the Huguenots based on toleration, which turned them into firm supporters of the monarchy. The church, however, was determined to introduce militant Counter-Reformation into Hungary, and Leopold I concurred, apparently agreeing with Philip II of Spain that a Jesuit convent was more effective than a military fortress.

The effects of this were decisive for subsequent Hungarian history. The harassing of the Protestants helped to throw the

42

entire population, already embittered by war requisitions and exactions of all kinds, behind the Hungarian magnates and gentry who rose in rebellion because their new King claimed the right to tax them. Within three years of the reconquest, all Hungary had risen against Habsburg rule in what in its early stages was a truly national and social revolution. Irregular bands of armed peasants and vagabonds, the dreaded *Kuruzen*, terrorized the areas which had only recently been devastated by the Turks, and engaged in effective guerrilla warfare a century before the Spanish peasants fighting against Napoleon gave us the term. The revolution failed in the end, but it destroyed whatever possibility there might have been of introducing absolute government in Hungary. By the Treaty of Szatmár (1711), the Hungarians recognized the Habsburgs as hereditary sovereigns, but Charles VI agreed to rule Hungary according

43

to Hungary's own laws. This put an end to the persecution of the Protestants, but an end also to any notion of taxing the Hungarian nobility.[22] The Habsburgs tried to recoup themselves by exacting a toll on all Hungarian exports to the rest of the monarchy, which had the unintended result of strangling industrial development in the kingdom. The failure to exploit Hungary's potential resources for the benefit of Habsburg power was thus compounded.

In these and other ways the wealth and power of church and nobility, so magnificently expressed in architecture and painting, frustrated the achievement of an adequate economic and financial foundation for the Habsburg monarchy's position as a great power. Any attempt to advance beyond the promising but as yet modest beginnings of economic growth described in the first section of this chapter, would have involved a challenge to the prevailing forms of feudal dominion and to the missionary Counter-Reformation priorities of the Catholic church. Significantly enough, there was a councillor in the Treasury (Hofkammer), a man in the mercantilist tradition introduced by Schröder, Becher and Hörnigk, who urged Charles VI to throw down such a challenge. In a long series of memoranda addressed to the Emperor, Christian Julius von Schierendorff proposed that burghers and peasants be given substantial representation in the diets in order to secure an equal distribution of direct taxation; that the lords should be compelled to lease their demesnes to the peasants so that all labour services could be commuted; and that the Protestants be granted toleration so as to provide much-needed stimulation to trade and industry.[23] Schierendorff thus anticipated in outline the reform programme of Maria Theresa and Joseph II, as well as that of Leopold II!

Why did Charles VI fail to take such splendid advice, which might have enabled him to escape the dire consequences of his country not being a sufficiently great power? The simple answer, often suggested, is that he followed too readily the contrary advice proffered by his father-confessor Tönnemann.

But before we accept this view, it is necessary to take a look at the state of the towns, that 'Fourth Estate' which Schierendorff clearly intended to call in to redress the balance in the Estates dominated by the privileged orders.

THE TOWNS

In central and eastern Europe, the seventeenth century had been a disastrous period for the towns. The development of the Atlantic trade-routes and the incursions from the east would in any case have brought them face to face with a long-term crisis. But any chance they might have had of adjusting themselves to the changed conditions was destroyed by the triumph of the Counter-Reformation and the effects of the Thirty Years' War. The inexorable choice presented to the Protestants by the Emperor Ferdinand II, of conforming to Catholicism or emigrating, resulted in the depopulation and rapid decline of numerous towns in Bohemia, Moravia and Austria. Silesia fared less badly, because Ferdinand's Catholic crusade was restrained there by international treaty obligations.

When the period of recovery set in after about 1660, the towns were no longer in a position fully to profit from it. In this period the landed nobility became the chief beneficiaries of economic recovery. They had transformed themselves from receivers of customary rents into demesne-farming entrepreneurs, selling corn, timber, livestock, wine and spirits. This 'fundamental agrarian revolution', as Professor Betts has called it,[24] created an expanding trade in agricultural produce which by-passed the towns. It was handled either by the nobles' own agents or by the Jews who were taking over the economic activities which had slipped out of the hands of the declining towns. Lady Mary Wortley Montagu, travelling through Prague in 1716, still gives an impression of unrelieved decline, describing a town 'for the most part old built and thinly inhabited', where those nobles resided who could not easily bear the expense of living in Vienna.[25]

In this dismal situation, the urban communities developed a narrow, restrictive outlook. Having lost the lucrative long-distance trade, they showed a fierce determination to minimize competition in the petty local trade and industry which still remained to them. This is the root of the growing obstinacy and exclusiveness of the guilds, the last survivals of former urban greatness. It is the root also of the strident anti-Semitism which became such a prominent feature of the urban mentality in Prague and Vienna. By appealing to Leopold I's Counter-Reformation fervour and reminding him of the expulsion of the Jews from Spain, the municipality of Vienna in 1669 instigated the decision to expel the Jews from the city.[26] The Treasury warned against the consequences of losing the important yearly sums received from the prosperous Jews in the form of the toleration tax and similar impositions. But the municipality

◀ 27 Prague in the early seventeenth century.

28 The expulsion of the Jews from Prague in 1745. According to the legend on this engraving, a 'secret cause' provoked the royal order, which affected 70,000 Jews.

eagerly promised Leopold full compensation, 'not doubting that Your Imperial Majesty will prefer to receive [the money] from Your most loyal . . . Christian and Catholic subjects rather than from the Jews, those blasphemers, murderers of God's son, hateful to all Christians and cursed by God and themselves'.[27] Needless to say, sheer financial necessity soon compelled the government to readmit a limited number of Jews, and this periodically provoked anti-Semitic outbursts of a most primitive nature from the municipality. These outbursts are perhaps the most striking illustration of the 'slough of despond' in which the towns of the Habsburg monarchy found themselves in this period.

But soon after the turn of the century, we can see the first signs of a revival of urban fortunes and of an impending crisis for the nobility and the church. Vienna had been spared the worst of the urban economic decline, because it had become the permanent Imperial residence and, therefore, the residence of the wealthier nobility also. The material requirements of the court and the palace-building nobility surrounding it were a considerable stimulant to the city's economy. As a result, the number of non-guild (*Hofbefreite*) artisans increased rapidly, despite the opposition of the guilds. By 1730 no fewer than seven factories existed in the new suburbs.[28] The city's orderly financial administration became the sheet-anchor of the monarchy's finances. The capital's first newspaper was successfully launched in 1703. In 1727 an unidentified entrepreneur attempted to launch a scientific-cultural periodical modelled on Thomasius's *Monatsgespräche*.[29] Two of Vienna's wealthiest burghers, both significantly architects, built for themselves palaces whose magnificent exteriors in no way reflected their owners' inferior social status, and a large number of ordinary burgher houses were built or rebuilt in a grand, palatial style.

In the late 1730s the municipality commissioned two works of art which were to express the city's new-found sense of dignity and self-confidence: a fountain for the courtyard of the Town Hall and another much more ambitious fountain for the great

9 Georg Raphael
Donner
(1693–1741).

Angel by Donner,
part of his work
for the Cathedral
of Bratislava.

31 The figure of Providentia,
symbolizing the virtues of the
municipal administration of Vienna,
from Donner's fountain in the
Mehlmarkt (Neue Markt).

square of the Mehlmarkt (now the Neue Markt). Both commissions were entrusted to the Austrian-born Georg Raphael
Donner, who quitted the services of the Primate of Hungary in
order to carry them out. When Donner had completed his
work, it could be seen that the municipality had chosen a
design which marked a fundamental break with the Baroque
tradition in sculpture. Ecstatic expressions and heroic postures
had yielded to a relaxed and inward stillness, which embodied
a new conception of greatness based upon a dignified simplicity.[30]
When Winckelmann later defined this new conception in his
famous tract[31] published in 1755, he was giving verbal expression to what Donner had already achieved in his work for
Vienna.

32 Giuseppe Galli–Bibiena's sumptuous décor for Johann Joseph Fux's opera *Angelica Vincitrice di Alcina*, a characteristic example of the impressive ostentation of the Baroque court theatre.

33, 34 Stage characters (noble Turk and cavalier) from the Baroque theatre.

35 Austrian actors preparing for a performance (*c.* 1700).

If we turn from the visual arts to drama, we find an analogous pattern of development. Characteristic of this period of the supremacy of the nobles was the decline of German as the literary language, and the dominance of Italian and French in its place. The court theatre was monopolized by Italian drama and opera, to which French comedy was added after the end of the seventeenth century. Apart from the plays (mainly didactic) of the Jesuits, drama in German was performed only by bands of strolling players, living from hand to mouth and performing in ramshackle huts or *ad hoc* premises. Soon after the turn of the century, however, the fortunes of the German theatre were beginning to rise.

Problems of space and congestion in the growing city had compelled the municipality of Vienna to undertake the building of a new theatre near the Kärntnertor. Though the court supported the claims of Italian companies, the new theatre had by 1712 become the permanent home of the German players.

This success was to a large extent the work of Joseph Anton Stranitzky, the *Prinzipal* (that is, director and chief playwright) of the German company and the creator of the Viennese popular drama. In Stranitzky's plays the Viennese population found its own authentic cultural expression, and this gave his company the strength to compete successfully with the Italian and French companies supported by the court.

Stranitzky took his dramatic source-material largely from libretti written for the Italian *opera seria* and from the Commedia dell'Arte. In his numerous adaptations he loosened the stiffly conventional style of the dialogue in these libretti, and heightened the emotional tension. His audience was evidently developing a taste for a wide range of emotional expression and for 'sentiment'. Into every plot he introduced the character of Hanswurst, which he always played himself. Descended from Shakespeare's clowns and other traditional comic figures, Stranitzky's Viennese Hanswurst was nevertheless an original character. Of peasant stock and employed in the service of the great, he expressed the plebeian point of view in a chorus-like running commentary on the thoughts and actions of the great. The comic element in his roles derives from the constant juxtaposition of the aspirations of the great with his own humbler and more earthy ambitions. By this device, Stranitzky was able to expose the occasional hollowness of the former as well as to assert the validity of the latter. The heroes were reminded of the plebeian Atlas on whose shoulders their world of impressive gestures and lofty emotions rested.[32]

This was not revolutionary drama. Hanswurst's insolence towards his betters did not symbolize a conscious rejection of existing social relations based on a vision of an alternative social order. Such a vision did not emerge until Rousseau's influence made itself felt much later in the century. But Hanswurst's insolence does indicate that in this part of Europe the spirit of the people remained unbroken, as was not the case everywhere else. The fiercest outbursts of outraged nobility were answered by Hanswurst with a phrase like 'so wird man ja noch reden

36 J. A. Stranitzky
in his famous
Hanswurst costume.

derffen' ('surely we can still *talk*').[33] And indeed, the Austrian public, in so far as we can judge, made good its claim to the right of free comment on social and political matters during most of the eighteenth century. As a comedian, Stranitzky was so successful that the Viennese nobility went to his performances as gladly as to the august presentations of the court. Lady Mary Wortley Montagu, who went to the Kärntnertor theatre in 1716, acknowledged that she had not laughed so much in her life, and that 'the people of the first Rank' who filled the boxes 'seem'd very well pleas'd with their Entertainment'.[34]

When considering the 'balance of power' between the nobility and the non-privileged classes, we must take into account the lack of homogeneity within the nobility. The period since the later Middle Ages had been one of increasing polarization between the great families, who could afford some

53

very ostentatious spending by the beginning of the eighteenth century, and the lesser nobility, whose real income was steadily declining. The fortunes of the lesser nobility (the Third Estate of the knights) resembled those of the towns more than those of the peers. The lesser nobles were, therefore, becoming increasingly dependent on employment by the state, if they wanted to maintain a standard of life 'befitting their estate'.

This increasing dependence is part of the background to the emergence in Europe of bureaucratic states and standing armies. The state employment sought by the lesser nobility – and, with the growth of entail, by the younger sons of the higher nobility as well – required a kind of training which the Jesuit institutions, with their near-monopoly of education, did not provide. Jesuit education was still founded on the neo-Scholastic *Ratio studiorum* of 1599, and was concerned with the doctrinal orthodoxy of all classes rather than with the vocational training of the lesser nobility. The inevitable result was that commoners, who possessed the required qualifications, often competed successfully for state employment. If they were Protestants, the requirement of prior conversion to Catholicism ceased to be an insurmountable obstacle as religious passion subsided. In some cases converts of 'base' origin attained the highest levels of government service. For the Habsburg principle was that their service required competent and experienced men, who were not so numerous that the government could afford to overlook them on account of their humble status.[35] Through such ability, Seilern, the son of a poor dyer in Ladenburg am Neckar, rose to the position of First Austrian Chancellor under Joseph I, and Bartenstein, the son of a Protestant professor at Strasbourg University, became Charles VI's principal adviser on foreign affairs.

Faced by this situation, the nobility was driven to a policy of self-help. Those nobles who could afford it sent their sons to Protestant universities abroad, where the modern subjects of public law, natural law and history were being taught by the greatest living authorities. Leyden was the most commonly

37 Kremsmünster Abbey, in which a noble academy was established, with its astronomical observatory.

chosen university. For those who could not afford to take this course of action, the Estates provided 'noble academies' (*Ritterakademien*), in which the above-mentioned subjects figured prominently in the curriculum. An academy of this type was established in the Abbey of Kremsmünster. The institution of chairs in natural law and history in the provincial universities was almost certainly due to the pressure of the nobility applied through the Estates.[36] The aim was to help the sons of the nobility to find honourable and lucrative government employment. But the more important result was that the new schools became the centres from which the philosophy of Leibniz and Wolff, and the ideas of the German Enlightenment, penetrated into the Habsburg monarchy.[37]

The social and cultural phenomena described above did not in themselves present a serious threat to the supremacy of the nobility or to the Counter-Reformation stance of the church. They do, however, help to explain why in the coming epoch the Habsburg rulers could meet the threat to the survival of the monarchy by a programme of reform embodying many ideas earlier put forward by Christian Julius von Schierendorff.

II CRISIS AND REFORM

THE CRISIS OF THE HABSBURG MONARCHY 1733–48

For a number of years the Habsburg monarchy succeeded in maintaining and consolidating the territorial gains of 1714 and 1718, and avoided stumbling too seriously in the ever-shifting sands of European diplomatic relations. In 1732, its international situation seemed satisfactory and secure. The Imperial Diet's vote in favour of the Pragmatic Sanction marked a revival of the Emperor's influence and prestige at the expense of France. Turkey was preoccupied with a war against Persia. Sardinia and Spain were unable to pursue their Italian ambitions without the aid of France. Charles VI had recently secured alliances with Russia and Prussia, and his suppression of the Ostend East India Company, a potential competitor of the English and Dutch East India Companies, had opened the way to a resumption of the traditional alliance with Great Britain and the United Provinces. The demise of this company frustrated all hopes of deriving full benefit from the possession of the Netherlands, but in the other provinces the government's mercantilist policies were beginning to show results.[1]

During the next few years, this situation changed dramatically for the worse. The monarchy, inadequately supported by its allies, had to face a formidable Bourbon challenge from across the Rhine and from Italy. As soon as this challenge was bought off by considerable sacrifices in territory and prestige, the monarchy drifted into an equally disastrous war with Turkey. When Charles VI died unexpectedly in 1740, the temptation to the powers to disregard the guarantees which they had pledged to observe the Pragmatic Sanction, and to deny Maria Theresa's right to her full inheritance, was irresistible because of the monarchy's evident weakness and disarray.

This remarkable reversal of fortunes was the result of defects both in the policies adopted and in the men chosen to carry them out. The problems involved in choosing a husband for an heir to a realm are notoriously difficult. Queen Elizabeth I of England had found indefinite spinsterhood the only satisfactory solution. Granted that such a solution was not open to Charles VI, nevertheless the marriages on which he decided for his daughter and the daughters of his late brother all helped to bring about, and to aggravate, the crisis of 1733 and the following years. The renunciations required from the daughters of Joseph I, when they were betrothed to the Electoral Princes of Saxony and Bavaria respectively, did not deter either of these states from envisaging claims to parts of the Habsburg inheritance, while the marriages themselves were bound to encourage them to do so. And Charles's increasingly obvious intention of making the heir to the Duchy of Lorraine his son-in-law was bound to be seen by France as a gratuitous provocation, putting a sudden end to her long-standing ambition of a gradual absorption of the Duchy. Charles's decision may have been the result of paternal indulgence, favouring a love-match, or of his impatience to become at least the grandfather of a male heir to the Habsburg monarchy, or of a quixotic impulse to rush to the defence of an Imperial territory to which he owed much. It may have been the result of a combination of all these motives. However attractive the motive, the stark consequence was the eclipse at Versailles of the peacefully inclined Fleury by the 'war party' of Chauvelin, who had little difficulty in finding a pretext for war and in mobilizing the enemies of the Habsburg monarchy in Italy and the Empire.[2]

Charles's alliances were as unfortunate as his marriage policies. Prussia alone offered adequate help in good time, but the State Conference thought it prudent to decline all but a small contingent, because the Prussian King's rapidly growing power and ambitions were beginning to arouse concern and jealousy in Vienna. Russia's help, on the other hand, was always late and inadequate, in effectiveness if not in numbers. Yet Austria felt obliged to repay it, and in trying to fulfil her obligations became involved in Russia's expansionist designs against Turkey at the most inopportune time. This was a feature of Austro-Russian relations throughout the eighteenth century, and was again to prove disastrous for Charles's grandson Joseph II. Britain's diplomats consistently outwitted Charles's ministers, and always managed to ensure that Austria met the French challenge where British rather than Austrian interests most required it (for example, in Poland in 1733 and the Netherlands in 1742), while urging Austria to surrender territories (for example, her Italian possessions in 1735 and Silesia in 1745) in favour of states which Britain was keen to appease.[3]

Such policies and failures indicate a modest level of capacity on the part of Austria's ministers and generals. It was surely no accident that the onset of the crisis coincided with the appearance of symptoms of senility in Prince Eugene. The majority of Eugene's colleagues in the government and the army command were of similar age to himself. When Mercy assumed command in Italy in 1733, he was nearly blind and deaf, and from time to time totally incapacitated. But he had to be killed in action before he was effectively replaced. Königsegg, who succeeded him, was not much younger, and failed disastrously. But he was given another chance of disgracing himself against the Turks in 1738, which he did. Sinzendorf, as Court Chancellor, and Seckendorff, as commander against the Turks in 1737, were not only incapable but of doubtful loyalty.

When Maria Theresa succeeded in October 1740, the level of morale in Habsburg governing circles was so low that nearly everyone seriously doubted the monarchy's chances of avoiding partition. When Frederick II's seizure of Silesia in December 1740 seemed to justify this pessimism, the leading ministers left the new, inexperienced ruler without counsel, because they wanted to steer a course suitable for all eventualities. Maria Theresa's determination to uphold the Pragmatic Sanction was supported only by Gundakar Starhemberg, who died in 1745, and by the outsider Bartenstein.[4]

The effort to secure adequate supplies for the armies moving up to meet the Prussian and Bavarian invasions was frustrated by the general reluctance of the nobility to make sacrifices for what they considered a lost cause, as well as by the determination of ministers to protect their own provinces from the burdens of requisitions and high taxation. In the provinces actually occupied by the Prussians and the Bavarians, the Estates submitted willingly and offered homage to their new masters. The ministers who owned land in Bohemia even asked Maria Theresa for permission to do homage to the Bavarian Prince in writing.[5] It is an odd paradox that in this desperate situation the only nobles who rose with some enthusiasm to defend the integrity of the Habsburg inheritance were those of rebellious, obstreperous Hungary.

38 An equestrian statue by Donner of St Martin, represented as a hussar. This was the most important work commissioned from the artist by the Primate of Hungary.

39 A statue by Messerschmidt of Maria Theresa, represented as King of Hungary.

By 1747 the country was on the point of exhaustion, most of the achievements of the previous reign had been undermined, and, though Bavaria had been subdued, there was no immediate prospect of the reconquest of Silesia. In these circumstances Maria Theresa reluctantly agreed to the Treaty of Aix-la-Chapelle (1748). It was the third successive treaty in which the Habsburg monarchy was compelled to make considerable territorial sacrifices. Since 1733 the monarchy had lost all its Italian possessions, save Lombardy, to the Spanish princes (Tuscany, compensation for Francis of Lorraine's lost patrimony, was administered separately), all lands south of the Danube and the fortresses of Orsova and Belgrade to the Turks, and Silesia (economically, its most advanced province) to Prussia. It was clearly losing the international race for power, in which an increasingly sharp pace was being set. To remedy this situation, Maria Theresa now turned to internal affairs with the object of securing what was so obviously lacking – an adequate economic basis to underpin her monarchy's status as a great power. In this field the Austrian achievement was to be unique.

ENFORCING A 'GOD-PLEASING EQUALITY'

The experience of the unsuccessful Silesian Wars aroused in Maria Theresa great indignation and a determination to remedy the most obvious weaknesses. These derived less from any inadequacy in the size of the armed forces than from the unwillingness and inability of the provincial Estates to provide adequately for their payment and supplies. The Estates' principal and consistent concern had been to minimize the burden on themselves and on their particular province, and they had been abetted in this concern by officials and ministers whose local and class loyalties outweighed all other considerations.

Maria Theresa decided to raise the subsidy (*Kontribution*) to be demanded from the provinces to the level required for the maintenance of a permanent military establishment of 108,000. The additional burden was to be met by subjecting seignorial land to taxation. A new land register was compiled for this purpose. At the same time, Maria Theresa was determined to ensure the efficient spending of the money collected. Hence the central government took over from the Estates the organization of the military contingents raised in their respective provinces. In this way, the increase in direct taxation came to involve a financial and administrative revolution of the first order. The function of the Estates was henceforth confined to collecting the land-tax as apportioned by the central government and finding the number of recruits asked for by the central government. To perform the now greatly extended governmental functions, a complete network of provincial and local government organizations was created, responsible to the new supreme Directorium in Publicis et Cameralibus, established in Vienna in 1749.[6]

The nobility offered fierce resistance to these changes, both individually and through the Estates. The leading ministers, above all the Supreme Chancellor Count Friedrich Harrach, acted as leaders of the noble opposition. Harrach submitted a plan by which the increased subsidy to be voted by the Estates would have been matched by a corresponding increase in the political influence of the Estates at the expense of the royal prerogative.[7] He and other ministers actively encouraged the opposition in the Estates to the royal demands. Maria Theresa's support came from the *parvenus*: from Bartenstein (the Secretary of the State Conference), from Koch (her Cabinet Secretary) and from Count Friedrich Wilhelm Haugwitz (a penniless Silesian émigré).

Haugwitz was the chief architect of the reforms, and almost single-handedly piloted them through the State Conference and the Estates. Though on one occasion he adduced 'the opinion of all political theorists' in support of his proposals,[8] his argumentation was not primarily theoretical. He justified the demand for increased taxes by reference to the new danger represented by Frederick II's Prussia, which he alleged to exceed the earlier dangers emanating from Turkey and France. He demonstrated the necessity of subjecting seignorial land to taxation by reference to the 'self-evident' inability of the peasantry to pay more than they were already paying. But he did reinforce these practical arguments by invoking a general principle of equity: 'As it is self-evident [*Landeskündig*] that the resources of the peasants do not suffice without the addition of the seignorial land, which is normally exempt from taxation, to defray the cost of the defence required for the security of the Crown and of the privileges of the Estates, both God-pleasing justice and natural equity demand that the nobility should contribute to this necessary defence in proportion to the full extent of their resources.'[9] Elsewhere in the document from which this quotation is taken we find the phrase 'God-pleasing equality', which may also be found in the writings of Schierendorff and can be traced as far back as the reign of Leopold I.[10] In the ranks of the noble opposition there was talk of an *esprit de nouveauté*, to which Maria Theresa had unaccountably succumbed, and bitter resentment that the sovereign should have heeded the advice of upstart secretaries and outsiders while ignoring that of her noble paladins.[11]

The political conflict over the proposed reforms was fought out with resourcefulness and determination on both sides. It is remarkable that Maria Theresa felt able to persevere in face of the almost unanimous opposition of the higher nobility, which enjoyed some articulate support among the people because of the increased burden of direct taxation which was involved.[12] The conflict with the ministers culminated in Harrach's refusal to present the royal propositions to the Lower Austrian Estates in his capacity as Governor of the province, and his resignation both as Governor and as Supreme Chancellor. In the negotiations with the Estates, Maria Theresa did not achieve a complete victory. Only those of Bohemia, Moravia, and Upper and Lower Austria agreed to the royal propositions in full. Elsewhere compromise agreements were reached. In Carinthia, the Estates – 'through ignorance or ill will', as Maria Theresa put it – resolutely refused to consider any means of raising the subsidy other than by increasing the burden on the peasants.

Here she proceeded to collect the increased subsidy *iure regio*, that is, unconstitutionally.[13]

All the same, the antithesis between monarchy and nobility should not be exaggerated. No one in the ministry or in the Estates disputed the need for the sums demanded. Apart from Harrach, no one offered an alternative to Haugwitz's plan for raising them. Moreover, the 'God-pleasing equality' invoked by Haugwitz was applied with due regard for noble privilege, and seignorial land was assessed for tax at a lower rate than peasant land.[14] The development of the centralized bureaucratic state machine, so offensive to the pride and political influence of the Estates, provided a much-needed field of honourable employment for the lesser nobility. Maria Theresa took great pains to enable the nobility to take advantage of the new opportunities. It was laid down that no one below the status of knight should be eligible for the new district captaincies.[15] The new academy for nobles in Vienna, the Theresianum (founded in 1749), and the new chairs of political science, history and natural law created in the course of the great university reforms of the 1750s, were to provide the vocational training required by young noblemen intending to enter government service, and complemented the educational efforts made by the nobility itself for a long time past. The prospect of state employment on this scale doubtless helped to reconcile the nobility as a whole to Maria Theresa's first reforms.

That the reforms on the whole achieved their object is beyond question. Kaunitz, in a sternly critical retrospective appraisal, acknowledged that they ensured the full and regular collection of the annual subsidies. In what has been called her 'Political Testament', Maria Theresa recommended the new system to her successors as the essential foundation of all good government. In doing so, she noted with particular satisfaction that, since the introduction of the new system, the provinces, instead of complaining of the excesses perpetrated by ill-paid troops, asked for the quartering of more regiments as a means of stimulating local trade.[16]

Nevertheless, the Third Silesian War, or Seven Years' War (1756–63), revealed the inadequacy of Maria Theresa's first instalment of reforms. After four years of war, the economy showed serious signs of strain, and many hopeful enterprises of the inter-war years lay in ruins. The increased revenue which had been secured was enough to cover ordinary peacetime expenditure, but not enough to cover even half the cost of the war. More than half the cost had to be covered by expensive loans which added enormously to the annual burden on the Treasury.[17] As the war progressed, the prospect of regaining Silesia receded, while the strain of continuing the war undermined the remaining resources of the state.

This crisis brought the State Chancellor, Prince Wenzel Anton Kaunitz, into the debate on internal policy. As the architect of the 'diplomatic revolution' which had ranged Austria, France and Russia against Prussia, Kaunitz considered that the collapse of the home front had deprived his diplomacy

40 Winter battle during the Seven Years' War: Austrian attack on a Prussian position on New Year's Day, 1757.

41 Prince Wenzel Anton Kaunitz (1711–94), Chancellor of State under Maria Theresa, Joseph II and Leopold II.

of the success which it deserved. He criticized Haugwitz's Directorium for uniting what should be separate and separating what should be united. This formidable attack naturally encouraged Haugwitz's old opponents and led to something like an aristocratic bid to restore the pre-1749 system. Kaunitz, however, stopped this offensive in its tracks by firmly dissociating himself from it, and making it clear that he was advocating a development rather than a revocation of the 1749 reforms. And in fact the result of the numerous administrative changes inspired by Kaunitz after 1760 was stronger central control over all matters connected with taxation and provincial finance. Though the Directorium was abolished, and the Court Chancellery (Hofkanzlei) and the Treasury (Hofkammer) were restored as separate ministries, the old provincial autonomy was not revived, while the new supreme Council of State (Staatsrat), set up in 1761, was intended to secure co-ordination in all matters of internal policy.[18]

Kaunitz was a member of the Council of State from its inception, and through it he was able to exert a strong and lasting influence on internal policy. Henceforward, Maria Theresa found in Kaunitz and the Council of State the ministerial backing for her reforming effort which had been so conspicuously lacking in the late 1740s. The enormous burdens which she had been compelled to impose on the people in order to finance the Seven Years' War compelled her after its conclusion to strive for an extension of the principle of 'God-pleasing equality' in the field of direct taxation. The reforms of 1749 had, after all, only marked a beginning. They had not, for instance, been applied to Hungary, because Maria Theresa had thought it inadvisable to attempt such a change in that country without calling a Diet, and the reaction of the Diet to such proposals was likely to be extremely hostile.[19] The Diet of 1751 voted a meagre increase of half a million florins in Hungary's disproportionately small annual subsidy, and this only in return for important and painful concessions. Now Maria Theresa was determined to make Hungary assume a fairer share of the vastly increased burdens. At the Diet convoked in 1764, the royal propositions were for an increase of a million florins in the regular subsidy, and the replacement of the personal obligation of the nobility to serve in the outdated feudal levy in time of war by a regular tax payable by lay and clerical nobility alike.

Maria Theresa knew that she would now encounter an aristocratic opposition far more formidable than any she had met in the 1740s. The Hungarian nobility was the most exclusive and articulate of any in Europe, and, even when refraining from rebellion, was prepared to stage an opposition argued out in the most elaborate constitutional terms. To meet this anticipated challenge, Maria Theresa and her advisers were concerned to provide some theoretical justification for the royal propositions. This appeared in the form of a book by the Hungarian scholar and custodian of the Imperial Library, Adam Franz Kollár, which refuted the well-known *thèse nobiliaire* embodied in Werböcz's commentary on the laws of Hungary, and asserted a full-blooded *thèse royale* with the help of an impressive knowledge of Hungarian history.[20] Two members of the Council of State seem to have been mainly concerned in commissioning this book, piloting it through the required censorship formalities and timing its publication to coincide with the opening of the Diet. But great care was taken to obscure the government's role, and to give the publication the appearance of a private initiative. The manœuvre is highly significant and illustrates the relationship between reforming absolutism and ideology, but it did not deceive the 1764 Diet, which unanimously refused to discuss the royal propositions until Maria Theresa had formally condemned and prohibited Kollár's book. Once again, a small increase in the subsidy was all that Maria Theresa secured, and this only in return for a formal withdrawal of the proposition for a tax to replace the feudal levy.[21]

Maria Theresa was more successful in securing a permanent basis for taxing the clergy. Hitherto, clerical taxation had depended on papal dispensations granted for a limited number of years and for specific purposes, such as the building of fortifications against the Turks. After the conclusion of the Seven Years' War, Kaunitz embarked on negotiations with the papal curia aimed at securing the extension of these dispensations for an indefinite period and without specification of purpose. Pope Clement XIII and his Secretary of State, Torrigiani, adopted an attitude similar to that of the Hungarian Diet, offering further dispensations only in return for concessions which would have opened the door to increased papal influence over the clergy of the Habsburg monarchy. The papacy was at this time gravely weakened by its conflict with the Bourbon dynasties over the expulsion of the Jesuits, and Maria Theresa, therefore, had no difficulty in successfully asserting a right to tax the clergy *propria auctoritate* (that is, without papal dispensation), and did so from the beginning of 1769. Nevertheless, as in the case of Hungary, great care was taken to provide full theoretical support for the monarchy's case. Rosenthal, the Imperial Archivist, was ordered to search for historical precedents, and found some dating from as far back as the fifteenth century. These precious documents were made available to Paul Joseph Riegger, the Professor of Canon Law at the University of Vienna, to serve as a basis for a learned publication justifying the rights claimed by the crown.[22]

INCREASING TAXABLE WEALTH

That the ultimate source of state power was an expanding economy and a prosperous population had been understood in Austrian governing circles since the appearance of the writings of the early cameralists. But it was not until after the Seven Years' War that the government in Vienna had the opportunity of embarking on a coherent legislative programme designed to raise the general level of the monarchy's economic performance. A long period of peace and an effective bureaucracy were indispensable prerequisites for the success of such a programme. The bureaucracy had been created by the administrative reforms of 1749, while Maria Theresa's pacific foreign policy after 1763 saved the Habsburg monarchy from involvement in a major war for the rest of her reign.

Clearly, the most important task was to improve the condition of the peasants. They were the foundation of the economy and the chief taxpayers, but there was an increasing demand for their forced labour for expanding manorial enterprises, both agricultural and industrial. Government interference in the relationship between lord and peasant would arouse fierce opposition on the part of the nobility at any time, but especially at a time of growing demand for peasant labour. Maria Theresa was determined to overcome this opposition.

When the Hungarian Diet of 1764 turned down the royal demands for a substantial increase in the subsidy, the reason put forward was the extreme poverty of the peasants. In her reply, Maria Theresa dropped a broad hint concerning the government's intentions: 'If the diet applied the appropriate means to further the welfare of the tax-paying population, Her Majesty does not doubt for one moment that the latter will . . . soon be in a position to discharge the increased tax-obligation which

42, 43, 44 Scenes of country life
in eighteenth-century Austria:
a peasant's farm and,
below, peasant women.

has been demanded.' The Diet ignored the hint, but after its closure Maria Theresa sent royal commissioners into Hungary to enforce a reduction of labour services *iure regio*. An *urbarium*, fixing a maximum scale of services equivalent to the existing minimum and by implication conferring the status of hereditary leaseholders upon the Hungarian peasants, was published as a royal decree in 1767.[23] As the administrative reforms of 1749 had not been extended to Hungary, it may be doubted whether this decree amounted to much more than a gesture outside the areas directly controlled by the royal commissioners.

Elsewhere, however, similar measures were being prepared under conditions providing the means for effective enforcement. In 1766 sporadic peasant unrest, and a widespread refusal by peasants to perform labour services, strengthened Maria Theresa's hand, as did the enthusiastic response which her objectives aroused on the part of some members of the new bureaucracy who were the products of the reformed universities. Franz Anton Blanc, serving on the royal commission investigating the peasant unrest in Austrian Silesia, emerged into prominence as a persistent advocate of radical reform. Against the lords' insistence on their inherited property rights, he asserted the principle of natural law that the peasant was entitled 'to sufficient food for himself and his family, to clothing and shelter, and to a reasonable surplus of these in case of a catastrophe'. Blanc's formulation served as the basis for the principle which Maria Theresa now laid down for the impending negotiations on labour services with the Estates: 'That the peasantry, as the most numerous class of society, which constitutes the foundation of the power of the state, must be maintained in a satisfactory condition, which means that the peasant must be able to support himself and his family, and in addition be able to pay his taxes in times of peace and war.'[24]

Negotiations on this basis were completed fairly quickly in Silesia and Lower Austria, resulting in 'Robot Patents' which limited labour services to a maximum of two days a week for full tenants and prohibited any increase on manors where cus-

45 Tobias Philipp Freiherr von Gebler (1726–86), statesman and playwright, member of the Council of State, where he vigorously championed the cause of Enlightened reform, from 1768.

tomary services had been less than the new maximum. In Bohemia and Styria, however, where large-scale demesne farming based on labour services was predominant, the determined opposition of the Estates delayed regulation by Robot Patents for several years. The nobles of these provinces were not inclined to surrender their inherited property rights in the name of natural law, and were strongly supported in their opposition by their respective provincial governments. Maria Theresa was supported by only a handful of councillors, including the recently promoted Blanc, at the Court Chancellery, and by Borié and Gebler in the Council of State. Reluctantly she agreed to a three-day maximum for these provinces, and did not feel strong enough to impose even this diluted reform until the widespread peasant rebellion of 1775 highlighted the possible dangers of leaving things as they were for much longer. A Robot Patent was imposed on Bohemia towards the end of that year, and on Styria in 1778; in both cases the Patents were imposed *iure regio*, without the concurrence of the Estates.[25]

The promulgation and enforcement of these Patents was the most serious challenge that any sovereign had yet dared to throw down to a socially powerful nobility. But after becoming thoroughly acquainted with the realities of feudal exploitation in Bohemia, Maria Theresa would clearly have liked to go further. In the Court Chancellery, Blanc now insisted on a compulsory general commutation of labour services as the only way of achieving the Empress's objectives. It is unlikely that he would have dared to do this if he had not been under the impression that the sovereign's intentions were tending in this direction. Even Joseph, Co-regent since 1765, felt that his mother was going too far and joined the opposition headed by the senior ministers. As a result, Blanc was demoted to the captaincy of a remote municipality, and Maria Theresa was compelled to confine further reforms to Crown and former Jesuit lands.[26] On these she established the system which she would have liked to enforce on all the private estates as well: the parcellation of the demesne among the manorial peasants on the basis of long-term leases. This was the system advocated by the cameralists as most conducive to peasant prosperity and agricultural improvement.

Quite as important as the new legislation was the fact that the administration created in 1749 was now in a position to enforce the long-existing legislation prohibiting the incorporation of peasant land in the demesne. After about 1775, the long-prohibited practice actually ceased, and some peasant land alienated since 1748 was restored to peasant tenure.

During these years, Maria Theresa was also engaged in a sustained effort to raise the level of industrial production in the monarchy. The ultimate objective was the same as that of the agrarian legislation – to increase taxable wealth. But in this case Maria Theresa came into conflict not with the nobility, but with the state credit institution, the *Stadtbank*. For the greatest obstacle to industrial development was the numerous heavy charges and duties of all kinds which were imposed upon all goods circulating within the monarchy. Most of these impositions were part of the state revenues, and some had been leased to the bank as security for state loans. The attempt, which was now made, to foster industry by abolishing or reducing the impositions therefore entailed the risk of at least a short-term deficit in the budget, and might undermine the stability of the bank. It was a newcomer, recently promoted to the Commission for Trade, the young Count Philipp Cobenzl, who gradually persuaded Maria Theresa and her advisers to take the risk for the sake of the long-term benefits. After Cobenzl had submitted a series of memoranda, the principle was accepted that duties must be regulated in accordance with commercial rather than fiscal considerations. This resulted in the suppression of numerous internal duties and the establishment in 1775 of a virtual customs union of the Austrian and Bohemian provinces, except Tirol. The duty levied on all exports from Hungary remained, because of the Hungarian Diet's refusal to pay a fair share of direct taxation. In relation to foreign countries, a highly protectionist policy was adopted; imports of goods were prohibited as soon as such goods or their equivalents were produced within the monarchy on an adequate scale.[27]

Great efforts were made to provide the commercial and industrial training needed so badly in a country taking its first major steps in industrialization. Village schools, especially in Bohemia, began to provide training in basic industrial techniques.[28] Prompted by the manufacturer Weinbrenner, the government established a School of Commerce (Realschule) in Vienna.[29] Joseph von Sonnenfels, soon to emerge as the leading economist of the cameralist school, was appointed to a new Chair of Administration and Commerce in the University of Vienna (1763). His most successful students were later appointed to similar chairs in the other universities. Eventually, the government helped to finance even art education through scholarships and the establishment of the Vienna Academy of Fine Art (1773), extending the policy of promoting home industries to the field of painting, architecture, and especially engraving.

This truly comprehensive effort to raise the level of economic activity was bound to affect the traditional relationship between the state and the Catholic church. The state now ceased to tolerate clerical and religious activities which appeared to impede important branches of the economy. Thus, in 1751, a complaint of the printers in Vienna about the serious obstacles created for them by the Jesuit censorship caused the government to take over the control of censorship from the Order.[30] The large number of obligatory saints' days, on which ordinary work was prohibited, was an impediment to production which seemed all the harder to tolerate because the Protestant countries were not subject to it. The government therefore sought a reduction in the number of sacred holidays, and obtained the agreement of the pope, who had earlier agreed to similar reductions in other countries. Significantly, the decree announcing the reduction contained clauses intended to promote increased religious observance on Sundays.[31] There followed decrees curtailing all ecclesiastical activities likely to tempt people away from productive work, and prohibiting transactions involving a drain of money abroad, whether this was due to the import of devotional etchings from Nuremberg and Augsburg or to the transfer of capital to monasteries outside the monarchy.[32] The church was being forced into the strait-jacket of cameralist economics.

UTILIZING WHAT THE CLERGY HAVE
Maria Theresa's 'Political Testament', written in about 1751, contains the following passage:

Here I shall say a few words about my predecessors. Their great piety led them to donate many, indeed most, of the Crown estates and revenues, which at that time served a good purpose in supporting religion and improving the position of the clergy. Since, however, God has now so blessed us in the German Hereditary Lands that both the Catholic religion is most flourishing and the clergy is sufficiently and well endowed, this principle is no longer valid. And I should therefore consider it not merely not laudable but rather culpable, if more property were to be given or transferred to the clergy. For on the one hand they do not need it, and on the

46 Maria Theresa and her family on the terrace of Schönbrunn palace.
Standing in the centre of the star pattern is Joseph, the heir to the throne.

other they do not, unfortunately, utilize what they have in the way they should, while being a heavy burden on the public, because no monastery remains within the limits set out in the terms of its foundation, and many idlers [*Müssiggänger*] are admitted. All this will require a great remedy, which I intend to undertake some time after due consideration.[33]

The search for the historical and ideological roots of what has come to be called 'Josephinian' church policy, in so far as it was not the result of purely mercantilist considerations, scarcely need go further than this passage. Precisely how Maria Theresa thought the clergy should have been utilizing its endowments may be inferred from what she did with the revenues of the ecclesiastical property which subsequently came into her hands. She endowed parishes and increased the provision of education, especially at the primary level. For all the vigorous applause which this drew from adherents of the Enlightenment, it is perfectly clear that she personally was most concerned with arresting the decline of Christian morality and Catholic orthodoxy which she believed to be evident in her territories. She also hoped to gain some political and economic dividends from an improvement in educational standards among her subjects. It is no less clear that she anticipated no major objections on the part of the papacy to the 'great remedy' which she intended to undertake. She began by submitting her proposals to the papal curia, clearly expecting papal approval, if not co-operation. This approval, however, was not forthcoming, though papal hesitation was probably tactically rather than dogmatically motivated. At the time when Maria Theresa made her proposals in the 1750s, the curia was thoroughly alarmed by the hostility of the Bourbon kingdoms, and feared that concessions to the Habsburgs would be eagerly exploited as precedents. In the light of the use which Kaunitz later made of papal concessions to the Wittelsbachs, it is possible that the curia's fears were not altogether groundless.

Be that as it may, Maria Theresa persisted with her reform plans despite the lack of papal approval. And this persistence added an ideological dimension to the problem. For it was now necessary to demonstrate the right of the state to interfere unilaterally in such ecclesiastical affairs as affected the interests of the state, the so-called *publico-ecclesiastica*. Inevitably, the argument about the merits of the planned reforms turned into an argument about the powers of the state. In this form it attracted all the passions and asperity which have traditionally characterized this particular argument, and which soon tended to overshadow the original concerns.

As a result, many historians have assumed (and some still assume) that the primary objective of Josephinian church policy was to establish the domination of the state over the church, and the term *Staatskirchentum* is frequently used in this connection. The term seems valid only if used to describe the means rather than the ends of Josephinism. Equally, I do not think we should be doing justice to the church's opposition, if we were to interpret it primarily as a struggle against Leviathan. The Catholic church had no objection to the extension of state power as such; its attitude depended on the way in which that power was exercised and the extent to which it was amenable to church guidance.

Historians who have concerned themselves exclusively with the form which the controversy assumed, postulate the existence, from the late seventeenth century onwards, of an Enlightened theory of absolutism which, during the eighteenth century, penetrated Catholic Austria, where it inspired a group of determined enemies of the church while also confusing the faithful. Such a theory, adhered to by Austrian Catholic historians from Albert Jäger to Ferdinand Maass,[34] signally fails to explain or to illuminate the historical phenomena. According to this interpretation, Maria Theresa appears to be alternately subject to the influence of the church's most dangerous enemies and to the promptings of her Catholic conscience and piety; Kaunitz to be arbitrarily drifting from a mood of compromise to one of

fierce determination to inflict maximum damage on the hated
church. It is only by constantly bearing in mind Maria Theresa's
original objectives that one can eliminate such inconsistencies
and confusions.

Maria Theresa made her first serious effort to put into effect
the 'great remedy' in church affairs within a few years of
writing her 'Political Testament'. The occasion, significantly,
was the discovery of widespread crypto-Lutheranism in Upper
Austria and Carinthia. To the pious, orthodox sovereign this
proved the urgent necessity of improving parochial work and
popular education, culpably neglected by the wealthy abbeys.
The plan was to draw upon monastic wealth in order to create
a 'Treasury of Religion' (*Religionskassa*) through which an
improvement and extension of parochial work could be
financed. One way of achieving this, which was seriously considered by the Directorium, was a reduction in the number of
monasteries through mergers. The proposal which Maria
Theresa's representatives at Rome submitted for consideration

was, however, the less radical one of a 10 per cent levy on the 'surplus' revenues of all monasteries. But even this failed to gain papal approval; and then the matter was overshadowed for some years by the Seven Years' War.[35]

When, in 1761, Maria Theresa was again able to give her attention to ecclesiastical questions, she was clearly determined to proceed unilaterally, as she later did in relation to clerical subsidies. To a report of the Directorium on church-state relations, submitted at the end of that year, she appended the following resolution: 'It is now quite clear that my House has allowed many rights to lapse in this and many other important respects. It is therefore necessary to think of appropriate remedies. This, however, is impossible, if all the circumstances are not known. Therefore the Directorium will have to see to it

48 Entry of Maria Theresa into Pressburg (Bratislava) in 1741.

that the necessary information and all the relevant documents are made available, and will have to suggest to me a competent individual to work on this material.'[36]

When this resolution was drafted, Maria Theresa's objectives had as little in common with the Enlightenment, and with rationalist theories of natural law, as they had had before the war. But the opposition of the papacy, and therefore of most of the clergy, compelled her to establish a case which, in the circumstances of the time, could be argued only in terms of the political theory of the Enlightenment. The 'competent individual' called for by the imperial resolution could only be a product of a Protestant university, or he might indeed have been one of the first graduates taught in the reformed law faculties of the Austrian universities. Jesuit-controlled education would not have provided him with the qualifications for this job. In fact, the work of establishing Maria Theresa's case in public was entrusted to Paul Joseph Riegger, Professor of Canon Law at the University of Vienna. The Empress rewarded him handsomely for his services, and ordered all teaching institutions in her dominions to adopt Riegger's books as the basic textbooks for the teaching of canon law.[37] It is remarkable how thoroughly Maria Theresa could divorce her personal inclinations from the requirements of her considered policies. The Jesuits, for whom she had considerable affection and respect, were gradually removed from their theological teaching positions, and in their place she appointed men whose general outlook was often fundamentally unpalatable to her, but whose services had become indispensable to the attainment of her objectives.

In 1762, Maria Theresa asked the reconstituted Court Chancellery to put forward proposals on how to reduce the excessive number of monks.[38] The Chancellery proceeded by the method which they had always adopted when this kind of question arose: by canvassing the opinion of the bishops. As a result, no proposals were advanced. This experience convinced the Empress that she needed a specialized ecclesiastical department in the Court Chancellery, which would be able to

49 Franz Joseph Ritter von Heinke (1726–1803), Secretary of the Ecclesiastical Department of the Court Chancellery. He was the most influential adviser on ecclesiastical affairs during the reigns of Maria Theresa and her sons.

formulate policies on ecclesiastical questions without consulting the leading clerical authorities. Schierendorff had advocated the establishment of such a department half a century earlier. Duly established in 1767, the new department was modelled on one which had already been functioning for some years in the Duchy of Milan. It was placed under the direction of Franz Joseph Heinke, a graduate of Halle University, where he had been a student of Christian Wolff.

The new department was given secret instructions, written by Kaunitz, which anticipated the positions which Maria Theresa intended to claim and establish through the legislation of the coming years. According to these instructions, the only ecclesiastical matters over which the state had no jurisdiction were those with which Christ had charged the Apostles, namely, preaching the Gospels, defining Christian doctrine, organizing the divine service and maintaining the internal discipline of the clergy. All other ecclesiastical matters were explicitly declared to be subject to the supreme jurisdiction of the secular authority.[39] Here was the framework for the 'great remedy' in church affairs. The instructions were wide enough subsequently to comprehend the entire ecclesiastical policy of Joseph II.

Now began the great series of decrees *in publico-ecclesiasticis*, a printed collection of which had to be kept for reference in every consistory and abbey. The most important of Maria Theresa's decrees were concerned with limiting the number of new entrants to, and the acquisition of further capital by, the monasteries. These were instructed not to exceed the number of inmates specified in the foundation charter (1767). No novice was allowed to take final vows before the completion of his twenty-fourth year (1770); vows taken at an earlier age were henceforth treated by the secular authorities as invalid. The 'dowry' brought to a monastery by a novice was limited to 1500 florins in cash or movables (1771). Numerous small and impoverished monasteries in Lombardy were suppressed. While the number of monasteries was being reduced and their size and wealth were being restricted, the government embarked on the task of aiding existing parishes, and founding new parishes throughout the lands of the monarchy.[40]

Maria Theresa's crusade to improve the standard of popular education may be traced back to a memorandum drawn up in 1769 by the Prince Bishop of Passau, calling attention to the continued existence of irreligion and the need for better schools. Her enthusiasm for this cause was echoed on many sides. Noble ministers remembered with resentment their own outdated and vocationally useless Jesuit education, while to adherents of the Enlightenment, like Tobias Philipp von Gebler in the Council of State, better education was the key to all human progress.[41]

Despite this enthusiastic consensus, Maria Theresa could not bring herself to disendow on her own authority a sufficient number of monasteries to finance a new educational system. For several years, therefore, her practical achievement was confined to the foundation of the Normalschule (a school planned as a model for other schools, and as a teacher training college) in Vienna (1771). But two years later, the suppression of the Jesuit Order by Pope Clement XIV gave her the opportunity to take the initiative. Supported by Kaunitz's vigorous diplomacy, she

50 The building which housed the main elementary school and teachers' training college (Normalschule) in Prague.

secured the reversal of the pope's original intention of retaining the property of the Jesuits in church hands.[42] Having achieved its conversion into state property, she used it to finance a comprehensive system of education in town and countryside throughout the lands of the monarchy. In parishes where no schools existed schools were established, existing parish schools were improved, and the smaller Jesuit grammar schools were converted into primary schools.

Maria Theresa took great care to ensure that the educational reforms should serve her principal objectives of strengthening the Catholic faith among her subjects and raising standards of morality. She rejected all proposals, no matter how desirable they might have been from a purely educational point of view, which seemed to her to entail the slightest risks to these objectives. Thus she rejected Pergen's proposal to remove the clergy altogether from teaching functions, though this compelled her to dispense with his valued services in the field of education.[43]

83

Her morbid suspicions also helped to frustrate Kaunitz's project of inviting renowned Protestant scholars from Germany to act as advisers in developing the new educational policies and curricula. Instead, she entrusted this task to Catholic clergymen who had successfully adapted the recent advances in education to the needs of Catholic schools. Abbot Felbiger of Sagan in Silesia was 'borrowed' from the Prussian King to organize the primary schools, and Gratian Marx, a member of the Order of Pious Schools, was put in charge of the grammar schools. As the approach of both men differed considerably from that of the new Commission for Education (Studienhofkommission), where the Enlightened ideas of Kressl and Martini predominated, Maria Theresa virtually excluded the latter from any further participation in the educational reforms except at university level. All the plans submitted by the Commission were shelved. The policy of Felbiger and Gratian Marx was to introduce the required improvements with the minimum change in either the traditional curriculum or the existing teaching personnel.[44]

If Maria Theresa seems to have imposed more radical reforms

51 Johann Ignaz von Felbiger (1724–88), Abbot of Sagan in Silesia, to whom Maria Theresa entrusted the direction of elementary education in all her hereditary dominions.

52 Franz Karl Freiherr von Kressl und Gualtenberg (1720–1801), to whom Maria Theresa entrusted the reform of university education and the administration of Jesuit lands after the dissolution of the Order.

53 Gerard van Swieten (1700–72), Boerhaave's most celebrated disciple, creator of the Vienna Medical School and Maria Theresa's most influential adviser on university reform and censorship.

on the universities than on the grammar and primary schools, there were compelling reasons for this. We have already seen how her wide-ranging programme of reform in the fields of finance, administration, commerce and relations between church and state involved the establishment of new university chairs and changes in the basic textbooks for most subjects taught by the faculties of law. Now, the 'great remedy' in church affairs, the massive redeployment of ecclesiastical effort from 'idle' monasticism to parochial work and popular education, required a radical reform of the theological faculties. For the existing Jesuit-controlled faculties were providing too many subtle scholars and too few of the energetic, practical men needed in the new parishes and schools.

It was the need for such men, and the growing estrangement from the papacy after its refusal to co-operate in the proposed ecclesiastical reforms in 1756, not the influence of her Dutch personal physician, Gerard van Swieten, or of any other individual, that brought Maria Theresa closer to the Jansenists and to the 'Reform Catholics' inspired by Ludovico Muratori.[45]

54 Franz Stephan Rautenstrauch (1734–85), Abbot of Braunau, Maria Theresa's and Joseph II's most important collaborator in the reform of theological studies.

55 Christoph Anton, Cardinal Migazzi (1714–1803), Archbishop of Vienna. Originally a supporter of ecclesiastical reform, he eventually became its most persistent opponent.

For various reasons, these factions within the Catholic church welcomed her plans for ecclesiastical reform with great enthusiasm, and eagerly offered their support. Their hostility to the popular cults and ceremonies of Baroque Catholicism, and their commitment to a simpler, more inward Christianity, led them to see in Maria Theresa, and later in Joseph II, true reformers of the church. Gradually, from 1759 onwards, Jansenists and Reform Catholics took over the control of the theological faculties and seminaries from the Jesuits and their followers. The Jansenist Bishop Simon Stock, appointed Director of the theological faculty of the University of Vienna, defined the principles in accordance with which theology would henceforth have to be taught. His successor as Director of the faculty, Abbot Stephan Rautenstrauch of Braunau, a leading Reform Catholic, elaborated these in a number of books which were prescribed as textbooks for all Austrian universities. Cardinal Migazzi, the Archbishop of Vienna, bombarded Maria Theresa with lengthy denunciations of dangerous

56 The new building for the University of Vienna, designed in 1753 by Jean Nicolas Jadot. ▶

heresies and falsehoods in the new teaching. The Empress unflinchingly supported the reformers, though she repeatedly rebuked them for the strident tone of factional controversy which tended to disfigure much of their writing.[46] A reference to the new theological teaching, in a report submitted by Heinke in 1781, gives us some idea of the changes which had been effected:

> All the aspects of the subject which have been neglected in the past are now taught – the basic history of the Church which was previously distorted by factionalism and *studia partium*, the art of scriptural interpretation on the basis of the original sources, literary knowledge of the best authors, the true use of the excellent Patristic writings, the art of preaching and teaching appropriate for convincing ordinary people, and finally a healthy moral theology corresponding to the word of God and a pastoral theology appropriate to the present time, in place of numerous and useless scholastic controversies.[47]

Theology had been pressed into the service of Maria Theresa's 'great remedy'. It had largely become vocational training for a new generation of parish priests and teachers.

DRAWING LOGICAL CONCLUSIONS: THE JOSEPHINIAN DECADE

On many occasions during Maria Theresa's reign, the consistent pursuit of her policies was sacrificed either to her own prejudices or to her practical political sense. After the Second Silesian War, which ended with the formal cession of Silesia to Prussia in 1745, she vented her hatred and frustration on the Jews of Prague, suspected of sympathy for the Prussians, by ordering their total expulsion from the city.[48] No action could have conflicted more fundamentally with the general policy, on which her government was embarking at that time, of encouraging commerce and industry. Likewise, she never considered a relaxation of the laws against heretics for the sake of achieving the economic benefits which she energetically pursued in other ways. All Maria Theresa's administrative measures and legislative enactments were modified to a greater or lesser degree to take account of local conditions or the strength of opposing vested interests.

When Joseph became Co-regent on the death of his father in 1765, he made this aspect of Maria Theresa's policies the chief target of his criticism. In a memoir of 1765 he wrote:

Great things have to be accomplished at one stroke. All changes arouse controversy sooner or later. The best way of going about it is to inform the public of one's intention at once, and, after having made one's decision, to listen to no contrary opinion, and resolutely to carry it out. All those who see only part of a problem cannot and should not discuss it. Every government measure is directed to the whole of a problem, every government action being related to the universal point of view, which only the sovereign and his most loyal servants ought to know and to act upon.[49]

Naturally, this abstract conception of the government's tasks frequently led Joseph to take up positions sharply at variance with those of his mother, with her cautious, experimental approach, and her tendency to be swayed by momentary impulse. The disagreement in the direction of affairs at Vienna became common knowledge in the other European capitals. Generally, Maria Theresa insisted on having her own way, and Joseph could do little except to express his frustration in letters to his brother Leopold, the Grand Duke of Tuscany.

Yet these were not wasted years for Joseph. Though he did not succeed in asserting his views against those of his mother, his duties as Co-regent brought him into close contact with all departments of government. He used this experience to work out in detail his own policies in readiness for the day of his accession, and was therefore able to embark on a many-sided reforming activity within weeks of his mother's death.[50]

The distinguishing feature of Joseph II's measures, after he became sole ruler in 1780, was their utter consistency. He did not introduce any new principles of government. But in accordance with the principles outlined in the memoir of 1765, he insisted on the complete and consistent application of the policies initiated since 1748 and contemptuously dismissed all contrary opinion. It would be a mistake to see in this only the fanaticism of an ideologue, or the outward expression of some psychological condition about the nature of which historians could only offer hypotheses. Certainly, Joseph's style of government suggests the schoolmaster whose sharp, authoritarian tone covers his lack of self-confidence. But such speculations can tell us little about the nature of his objectives. More relevant to these was the fact that the targets for military strength worked out in 1748 had to be revised upwards after the Seven Years' War. Maria Theresa had set out with the aim of creating the administrative and economic foundation for a permanent military establishment of 108,000 men. After 1763 her government maintained an establishment of 300,000 men. During the years of his co-regency, Joseph became increasingly obsessed by his realization that the monarchy was far from having achieved an adequate foundation for an army of this size. It was in fact maintained by the continuation in peacetime of all the additional taxation imposed during the Seven Years' War, a makeshift measure which undermined the effectiveness of the government's entire programme of reforms, and helped to bring about economic catastrophe in Bohemia in the early 1770s and the near-collapse of the entire economy during the War of the Bavarian Succession (1778–79). These two crises must have served to confirm Joseph in his critical attitude, and to reinforce his fierce and determined consistency. 'Our provinces are impoverished,' he wrote in 1779, 'and cannot afford to maintain the present military establishment . . . only the improvement of our agriculture, industry, trade and finance will make possible the upkeep and expansion of our military forces to meet future eventualities.'[51]

57 The peasants' Emperor. Joseph II behind the plough, a scene frequently reproduced in subsequent years.

58 Joseph II and his brother Leopold in Rome in 1769. ▶

Already after his journey through famine-stricken Bohemia in 1771, Joseph had expressed his concern at the limited and inconsistent manner in which Haugwitz's reform of direct taxation had been carried out. He was willing to tolerate neither the incomplete land register compiled in the 1750s and 1760s, from which much productive land had been omitted, nor the inequality of the tax burden as between lord and subject and as between different provinces. He therefore insisted on advancing from Haugwitz's cautious steps towards a 'God-pleasing equality' to the introduction of a uniform land-tax based upon a complete land register. This constituted the main item in the programme of financial reform which he outlined in a letter to the Supreme Chancellor, Kollowrat, at the beginning of 1783.[52] The project bristled with every kind of difficulty, from the lack of qualified land-surveyors and statisticians to the almost unanimous opposition of the higher ranks of the bureaucracy. Joseph contemptuously rejected his opponents' arguments, which seemed to him to be based on ignorance and selfishness. The bulk of the enormous work entailed in compiling a new land register, and in estimating average yields, was done by some enthusiastic reformers in the lower ranks of the bureaucracy and by peasants who thereby refuted the prevailing legend of the universal dull-wittedness of their class.[53] Friedrich Eger, the son of a non-noble minor official, rose to high ministerial rank on account of his ability to put Joseph's ideas on this and related reforms into practice. The Emperor was even unwilling to make allowances for the special status and conditions of Hungary, and replaced the entire constitutional administration in order to make sure that the preparatory work would be carried out in the kingdom. As the task of calculating net income from land proved beyond the capacity of the bureaucracy, it was decided to make gross yields, calculated on a ten-year average, the basis of tax assessment, and to impose the relatively low rate of taxation of 12 per cent.

Opponents of the reform invoked the unreliability of a land register based on measurements carried out by semi-literate peasants, but recent research has shown that later nineteenth-century surveys did not produce significantly different results.[54] The Josephinian survey certainly brought to light a great deal of land which had not been included in the Theresian one. The reform deprived the privileged orders of the last *de facto* remnants of their immunity from direct taxation. It was also going to deprive the Estates of one of their last surviving practical functions, because the reformers considered the manorial tax-collectors unqualified and unsuitable for the collection of the new tax. They had no difficulty in persuading Joseph to appoint state tax-collectors throughout the lands of the monarchy. These began the work of collecting the new tax on 1 November 1789, four months before Joseph's death.

Although Joseph had not supported his mother's impulsive attempts in the late 1770s to enforce a general commutation of labour services on all manorial estates, the preparatory work on the land-tax made him reconsider this question. On the one hand, the bewildering variety of traditional obligations made the work of calculating income from land extremely complicated; on the other hand, if every land-holder was in future to pay a 12 per cent tax to the state in addition to his local obligations, and was still to be able to maintain himself and his family in a 'satisfactory' condition, there was not much room for variation in the rate of feudal exploitation. In the light of the cameralist teaching about the importance of a prosperous, self-respecting peasantry, Joseph concluded that the peasant must be allowed to retain at least 50 per cent of his gross income for his own and his family's sustenance. He thus laid down the 'inviolable and glaringly obvious principle of justice' that the combined burden of state tax, feudal dues, village contributions and the cost of cultivation must never exceed 50 per cent of the gross annual yield of a peasant's holding.[55] Given a land-tax of $12\frac{2}{9}$ per cent and an estimated 20 per cent for village contributions (towards the support of the parish, the schoolmaster, and so on) and the cost of cultivation, there remained a maximum of $17\frac{7}{9}$ per cent of the gross yield as the share of the lord. The

February Patent of 1789, which introduced the new land-tax, duly established this percentage as the maximum which a lord could require from his land-holding subjects. Furthermore, it was normally to be paid in cash.

The new regulation of feudal dues was a much greater blow to the nobility than the uniform land-tax, especially in the provinces, where large-scale demesne farming based on labour services prevailed. In Galicia, the Polish province acquired by Austria under the terms of the First Partition in 1772, the new maximum represented in some cases no less than a 60 per cent reduction in feudal dues.[56] Anticipating economic ruin, the nobility roused itself to determined opposition, which resulted in some wavering among the reformers and secured two last-minute concessions. Peasants settled on seignorial land – generally the poorer sections of the peasantry – were specifically excluded from the benefits of the new maximum, and the lords of Bohemia and Galicia were allowed to exact labour services for one and two more years respectively after the coming into force of the decree, in order to facilitate the process of readjustment. In these provinces, therefore, the February Patent had not yet fully come into force by the time it was repealed in April 1790.

Joseph seems to have enjoyed pitting his wits against those of his ministers in the lengthy arguments about the reform. His contributions to the dispute show that he conceived the reform as a massive incentive to agrarian improvement. He adopted the cameralist theory that a prosperous peasantry enjoying security of tenure was the best guarantee for efficient and expanding agricultural production. The nobility's fears of ruin under the new maximum he dismissed as evidence of their inefficient estate management: let the lords parcel out their demesnes to hereditary leaseholders as the Crown had done, and all would benefit. Joseph's other agrarian legislation was similarly designed to help the peasants fulfil their potential as efficient tillers of the soil and as reliable subjects and tax-payers. The abolition of servile status and its outward manifestations

59 The Neue Markt, Vienna, seen from the south.

(1781), and the improvement in the peasants' security of tenure (1789), were intended to boost peasant morale and initiative, and doubtless did so.[57]

Needless to say, the majority of the nobility did not share the reformers' estimate of peasant character and potential, and predicted that their subjects would merely waste the greater free time that the reforms would give them. But for the sake of the great economic advantages which he confidently expected to ensue, Joseph was prepared to throw down a direct challenge to the most powerful group of his subjects united in opposition against him. If Joseph could deal with obstinately defended feudal privileges in this way, what chance was there for any other institutions or traditions which seemed to stand in the way of the full realization of the monarchy's economic potential, especially if they were less powerfully defended? For the sake of the economy, everyone willing and able to serve the monarchy must in future be free to do so in the capacity for which he was best qualified. Guild restrictions contravening this fundamental rule were not tolerated. Nor was the Counter-Reformation heritage of enforced confessional uniformity which had been the core of Habsburg internal policy for two centuries. To Maria Theresa its maintenance had been a duty to God which outweighed all other considerations. But Joseph II's god was a cameralist god: 'The service of God is inseparable from that of the state, and God wants us to utilize those whom he has endowed with talents and capacity for business, leaving the reward of good and the punishment of evil to his divine mercy.'[58] Maria Theresa shuddered at the very word 'toleration'. But Joseph refused to discuss the question in any but economic terms: 'To me, toleration means only that in purely secular matters . . . I am prepared to employ anyone, let anyone practise agriculture or a trade, or establish himself in a city, who has the required qualifications and would bring advantage or industry into my states.'[59]

This matter remained a source of disagreement between mother and son until Maria Theresa's death. As sole ruler, Joseph II immediately ordered the authorities to end repression and discrimination against adherents of the Lutheran, Calvinist and Greek Orthodox faiths. As the change was not ideologically motivated, and no attack on the position of the 'dominant' church was intended, Joseph hoped to carry out the change without formal legislation and with the minimum of publicity. But rapidly developing rumours and speculation about the extent of the new toleration compelled Joseph to publish the famous Patent of Toleration (1781) in order to make clear the limits of his policy. The Patent offered a rather grudging and limited toleration to the religions mentioned above. The clergy were instructed to propagate the faith without insulting the adherents of the other tolerated denominations. Joseph was scrupulously concerned to keep his policy within the limits of what Catholic theologians call 'civil toleration', and not to allow the free competition of all views on an equal basis. Everyone who took advantage of the Patent to register as a non-Catholic had to opt for one or other of the tolerated denominations. The Bohemian peasant heretics who were quite sure that they were neither Lutherans nor Calvinists were in the end dealt with in much the same manner as they would have been under Maria Theresa; that is, they were forcibly transported to Transylvania.[60] Significantly, however, Joseph was prepared to go beyond the provisions of his own patent, if the economic objectives underlying his policy required it. In 1784 the question arose whether some Mennonites from Germany, who wanted to settle in Galicia (a province much in need of industrious settlers), should be allowed to do so. The Court Chancellery, sticking to the letter of the Toleration Patent, turned down the application. But Joseph resolved that the application should be granted, 'if [the settlers] are good tillers of the soil'.[61]

It must be emphasized in this connection that Joseph did not share his mother's hatred and contempt for the Jews, though by the 1780s there had as yet been little decline of anti-Semitic prejudice among the poor of town and countryside. Hence Joseph believed that, given some encouragement and education, this tormented and humiliated section of his subjects might make a greater contribution to the economy than the existing discriminatory and oppressive legislation allowed it to make. And he was not prepared to wait for a change in the popular attitude towards the Jews before making the necessary changes. Already in May 1781 he revealed his intentions in a letter to the Court Chancellor; in order to make the numerous members of the Jewish community more useful to the state, he was considering admitting them to the public educational institutions, letting them carry on agriculture and industry, and allowing them to enter the professions if they had the necessary ability and training. The body most immediately concerned, the Lower Austrian government, reacted to the Emperor's proposals with barely concealed hostility. But there was enthusiastic support for them from Greiner in the Court Chancellery and Gebler in the Council of State. The Patent, finally issued at the beginning of 1782, contained some concessions to popular prejudice, but gave effect to most of Joseph's intentions. Most of the existing restrictions relating to the Jews were removed, to give them the opportunity and incentive to develop and practise their varied talents.[62] An effort was made to ensure that popular prejudice should not frustrate the objectives of the new legislation, as may be seen from the following instruction to teachers, drafted by Sonnenfels:

> The purpose [of the Patent on the Jews] would be largely frustrated, if [Jewish] parents had cause to fear that their children would be maltreated in school, or that their religious faith would be undermined there. Teachers are therefore instructed to be polite to the parents who come to see them, and to reassure them that higher instructions fully protect their children in relation to both these matters. . . . Teachers will not only set their pupils an example of decent and peaceful behaviour by their own impartiality and kindness, but will also exhort their pupils from time to time to behave in a similar way, and will inflict conspicuous punishment on those who act differently.[63]

State-imposed religious conformity and deep-rooted popular prejudice both had to yield to Joseph II's cameralist crusade.

Protection, the most direct method of fostering a backward economy, had been the rule under Maria Theresa. But dispensations and special licences had often been granted in contravention of the general policy. Here, too, Joseph was consistent and went to the logical extreme of prohibiting the imports of those manufactures whose home production he was most concerned to encourage. The British Ambassador, Sir Robert Murray Keith, had to report to his government that Joseph's logical consistency ruled out the possibility of any exception in favour of Great Britain, whose exports were of course seriously affected. 'These regulations,' he wrote, 'make a part of His Majesty's Plans for the Encouragement of the National Industry. They are intended to be permanent.'[64] Sir Robert knew how single-mindedly Joseph was pursuing the objective of encouraging national industry, and how many formidable nettles he had already grasped for its sake.

Historians have for some time recognized the continuity between Maria Theresa's and Joseph's ecclesiastical policy. But often this continuity is understood in the sense that the hostility to the church attributed (wrongly in my opinion) to Joseph II is seen as a determining factor in his mother's ecclesiastical legislation. There is, however, overwhelming evidence of Joseph's genuine and devout Catholicism, though it was of a distinctly more Jansenist-Muratorian character than that of his mother.[65] He was, therefore, closer in outlook than she had been to the civil servants in the ecclesiastical department of the Court Chancellery and to the clerical supporters of reform. The vital point, however, is that he shared his mother's view that the church was not putting its great wealth to the best use. His impatience with the existing priorities of the ecclesiastical hierarchy grew as he became increasingly aware of the necessity for more far-reaching reforms in the state. After he had witnessed the Bohemian famine in 1771, he impatiently called for the 'great remedy' projected by Maria Theresa in her 'Political Testament':

In Bohemia alone the clergy own one-seventh of all the land . . . in Moravia perhaps more, and it is said that endowments . . . amount to eight million florins. What a rich source for the suppression of mendicant monks, the establishment . . . of a true hierarchy, the furthering of religion in accordance with the true dignity of our creator and saviour – what resources are there for the most salutary institutions, additional parishes, teachers, seminaries and houses for retired clergy, for foundling homes, orphanages, schools, workhouses, remand homes, prisons and hospitals! . . . All this would

99

surely be more appropriate to the perfection of God than the present inactive life of most monasteries, yes, even of bishops and parish priests. All are servants of God, like ourselves – but also of the state. It is our task to see to it that they fulfil their duty. . . . That has nothing to do with dogma, rites or morals. How shameful are the two cases which have recently occurred in Prague: in this year's famine five or six people have actually died in the streets, and many more have fallen ill and have taken the last sacrament in the streets. Some charitable citizens at last took them into their houses. . . . In this city, where there is a rich archbishop, a large cathedral chapter, so many abbeys, three Jesuit palaces, so many monks, there is not a single proven case that any of these took in one of the miserable wretches who were lying in front of their doors. . . . And more, a battalion . . . was recently transferred to Prague, but as its staff stayed behind, they did not have their chaplains with them. Some of the soldiers fell ill. A priest was asked for in all the monasteries and none was found. . . . At last a secular priest who had once been a soldier offered to hear confession and aid the dying man.[66]

Whether or not these stories were exaggerated, the verisimilitude of the general situation depicted need not be doubted. Joseph was, moreover, appalled by the popular ignorance and superstition which he encountered. It seemed intolerable that hundreds of clergymen, instead of improving popular education and morals, should congregate in the capital and make a living by reading Masses for anyone who paid them half a florin for the service. And what could many of the clergy actually do for education, seeing that they were themselves only 'consecrated peasants', many of whom spent much of their time managing the parish farm? Joseph did not believe that, in a situation such as this, his mother's piecemeal approach would have achieved anything worth while: 'What is the use of the partial measures for the improvement of the clergy taken by our miserable Commission for Religion? What is the significance

60 From the 'Gallery of Catholic Abuses': a Mass with orchestra, *primo buffo* and *prima donna* in the Cathedral of Vienna. The Reform Catholics preferred silent devotion and simple hymns for the whole congregation.

of a holiday more or less, or of a few nuns?'[67] Joseph wanted to see the power of the state used to enforce a major redistribution of clerical wealth and functions and a comprehensive reform of clerical education.

As sole ruler, Joseph drew back from the programme of total control and total reform which he had worked out for himself as co-regent. Heinke warnèd him of the formidable difficulties and doctrinal problems involved. But the pace of reform *in publico-ecclesiasticis* quickened considerably. Foreign jurisdiction over sections of the church in the Habsburg monarchy was terminated. Insignificant malpractices in a Carthusian monastery were seized on to provide the opportunity of decreeing the dissolution of all contemplative monastic Orders (1782). Their property was used to endow a fund (*Religionsfond*) from which additional bishoprics and parishes were maintained. A portion of the fund was devoted to providing a regular pension for mendicant monks and friars, in order to put an end to the begging which had long been regarded as an intolerable burden on the heavily taxed rural population. The number of mendicant houses was reduced by mergers. But Joseph soon realized that he had over-estimated the resources of the dissolved monasteries, and he therefore proceeded to dissolve individual wealthy houses of Orders which he did not intend to suppress *in toto*, in order to keep the *Religionsfond* solvent, while the surviving wealthy houses had to contribute their 'surplus' revenue to the fund. In the Austrian provinces alone, 150 monasteries were suppressed, and their revenues were devoted to the maintenance of over 600 additional parish clergy. The aim was to create parishes of not more than 700 people, and to ensure that no one lived more than one hour's walk away from his parish church.[68]

Joseph was concerned with the redeployment of the human, no less than the material, resources of the monasteries. The majority of the monks from the suppressed monasteries, who were not too old, were transferred to parish work or took up teaching. The surviving monasteries were told in no uncertain terms that in the Emperor's eyes they were communities of parish clergy. They were, therefore, to refrain from any activities likely to impair their health and energy, and thus likely to render them incapable of carrying out their allotted functions. Loud choral singing, stated a decree of 1786, had been medically proved to constitute a serious hazard to health, and should therefore be replaced by quiet singing, or, better still, by spoken prayer.[69]

The difference between the suppression of monasteries under Joseph II and that which had taken place under Maria Theresa lay not only in the different scales of the two operations. Though Maria Theresa could have proceeded unilaterally under the principles of church-state relations which she had laid down, she had in fact dissolved monasteries only after obtaining the pope's prior sanction. Joseph made no attempt to secure such sanction, doubtless feeling certain that it could not be obtained for the very considerable number of monasteries that he had in mind. The pope, on the other hand, though he failed to obtain any material concessions by his sensational trip to Vienna in the spring of 1782, did not condemn Joseph's action retrospectively. In view of the use to which the suppressed monasteries' income was being put, it would have been difficult for him to do so.

The complete reorganization of the education of intending clergymen was the logical extension of Joseph's ecclesiastical reforms. The majority of the higher clergy, both secular and regular, had reacted to the reforms with such undisguised hostility that Joseph could not possibly expect to obtain the parish clergy he so ardently desired from the monastic schools or the episcopal seminaries. Earlier decrees, requiring monasteries to base their theological teaching on the books prescribed by Abbot Rautenstrauch for the theological faculties of the universities, had remained dead letters.[70] Joseph was, therefore, easily persuaded that the monastic schools must be abolished altogether. The problem of their replacement gave rise to a significant disagreement between Joseph and his councillors in the ecclesiastical department. The latter, especially Kressl, President of the Commission on Ecclesiastical Affairs, proposed that all intending monks and priests should simply be required to attend the recently reformed courses in theology at the universities as ordinary students. But Joseph thought that the high moral qualities which he wanted to see in his parish priests might be nipped in the bud by the temptations and excesses of five or six years of student life. It was with these moral qualities in mind that he conceived the idea of state-supervised General Seminaries in which intending priests and monks would live separately from the general body of students while pursuing their theological studies at the universities, and in which their studies could be supplemented by a practical moral education. To Kressl's objection that segregation would prevent intending priests from acquiring the necessary practical knowledge of men and the world, he replied:

> The General Seminaries . . . have the following purpose: complete uniformity of theological and moral teaching, and the closest supervision over the moral development of the young men intending to enter the priesthood. After the completion of his philosophical studies, the intending priest is about sixteen or seventeen years old . . . when it is to be hoped that his morals are still unspoilt. Now, to keep this young man away from danger during the first difficult period of developing adolescent passions, and at the same time to instil into him such principles as will later, reinforced by six years' study, help him to maintain his moral standards, for this I consider communal life in seminaries essential.[71]

This interesting passage tells us perhaps as much about Joseph as an individual as it does about the motivation of his reform.

General Seminaries, though opposed by bishops and reformers alike, were set up in nearly every provincial capital. Rautenstrauch, who, like Kressl, had opposed them, nevertheless agreed to draw up their constitution and order of studies. Overwhelming emphasis was placed on training priests who would be able to cure souls and provide some basic education in every part of the lands of the monarchy. We may detect Joseph's rigorous consistency again in the fact that these seminaries became the first modern institutions in which all the languages spoken in the lands of the monarchy were used and taught. Though the seminaries did not survive for many months after Joseph's death, the gigantic shift of ecclesiastical resources and activity in the direction of practical parish and educational work was irreversible.

The crisis of the Habsburg monarchy and the traumatic shock of the loss of Silesia had provided the stimulus for the most remarkable and sustained programme of reforms which any European country had yet attempted to achieve in so short a time. Maria Theresa's determination, temperament and strength of character enabled her to adopt new and untried policies, and Joseph's open, logical mind and rigorous consistency impelled him to give general application to his mother's policies and to develop them to their logical conclusion. Both were prepared to abandon hallowed traditions and to stand up to widespread and fierce opposition from the vested interests whose privileges conflicted with the objectives which they had set before themselves. They were able to do so because they found support among a group of men, educated at Protestant or at reformed Catholic universities, who eagerly persuaded themselves that the new policies were the first instalments of a great social transformation undertaken as a result of the growing influence of the Enlightenment. In organizing this support, Maria Theresa and her son helped to bring these men to the centre of affairs, and some of them were able to attain high ministerial rank. By no means all of the objectives that Maria Theresa and Joseph II had set themselves were achieved, nor was the opposition ultimately overcome in every case. But enough was achieved to initiate social and cultural developments in the course of which the peoples of the Habsburg monarchy shook off a good deal of the stagnation which had been the legacy of the Counter-Reformation. In doing so, they inevitably became susceptible to the disturbing and stimulating influences of the Enlightenment. Not all the consequences of this had been either intended or foreseen. In fact, the Habsburg monarchy had overcome one crisis only at the price of creating another.

61 The celebration of the wedding of Charles of Lorraine to Archduchess Marianne in 1744, one of the last great court festivities of the Baroque era.

III SOCIAL AND CULTURAL DEVELOPMENT

ECONOMIC GROWTH AND SOCIAL INTEGRATION

The government's persistent efforts to stimulate the economy met little success before the Seven Years' War. The home market remained too restricted. The products of Austrian factories were generally spurned as too expensive and inferior to foreign imports.[1] Consequently, many intending manufacturers (if they did not, like the Emperor Francis I, own a personal fortune) went bankrupt, despite extensive privileges and generous financial assistance.

From the end of the Seven Years' War, however, the tide began to turn. Industrial production of all kinds began to expand. An increasing proportion of newly founded factories survived, and the few old-established ones increased their work-force. Gradually the products of Austrian factories ceased to be regarded as suspect oddities. Monopoly rights (*privilegia exclusiva*) no longer seemed essential for the success of new undertakings. Already in 1764 the most important branches of manufacture, woollen and cotton goods, were declared free to all who cared to try their hand at them.[2] Most factories henceforth were 'privileged' only in that they were exempted from all guild restrictions and from the liability of quartering troops.

Not only was the volume of production increasing; there were also important qualitative changes in the social relations of production. Firstly, factory-based production was increasing at a relatively greater rate than traditional artisan production under guild control. Secondly, the founding fathers of Austrian manufacture, the manorial lords with factories on their estates manned by the labour of their own feudal subjects, were now being overshadowed as industrial entrepreneurs by bankers,

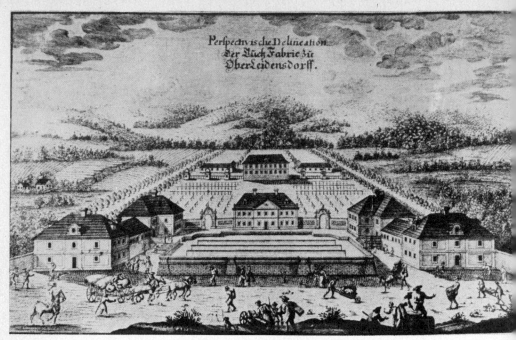

62 Textile factory in Oberleidensdorf, Bohemia (1728).

merchants, high officials, and occasionally even successful craftsmen. Thirdly, work organized under one roof in the factory building grew in importance in relation to work put out to domestic workers in villages or to the inmates of poorhouses. Some factories now accommodated a thousand workers under one roof and operated an advanced system of specialization.[3] Though the introduction of power-driven machinery did not take place until the nineteenth century, the foundations of the industrial revolution were already being laid.

After Joseph II's accession in 1780, the rate of industrial development quickened considerably. The abolition of serfdom, the Patent of Toleration and the dissolution of the monasteries all stimulated industrial enterprise in different ways. The virtual prohibition of imported manufactures imposed in 1784, the culmination of forty years of cameralist efforts, encouraged almost overnight the foundation of new branches of the 'national' industry. In Lower Austria, which during this period replaced Bohemia as the most industrialized province of the Habsburg monarchy, the number of people employed in industry was nearly doubled in the short period from 1783 to 1790. By the latter date, a total of at least 280 factories were operating in the monarchy (excluding Hungary), half of them in Lower Austria.[4] There were a hundred or so in Vienna and its region which produced all the articles in common use at the time. A good indication of what was being achieved in the field of industrialization, and a measure of the international recognition of that achievement, was the fact that, in the 1780s, finished goods accounted for 65 per cent of the monarchy's exports and only one-sixth of its imports.[5]

From the mid-1780s, Austrians began to feel and express the confidence that the Habsburg monarchy had entered the ranks of the industrialized countries. The Emperor himself, who was

63, 64 Scenes of early eighteenth-century Bohemian mills (*Manufacturen*), in which traditional implements were assembled in fairly large numbers under one roof: right, a factory of looms, below, spinning wheels.

65 Austrian peasant chest. This type of splendidly decorated furniture was the most common evidence of eighteenth-century peasant prosperity.

not given to over-estimating the extent of his own achievements, expressed his pride in a letter to his brother, Leopold of Tuscany: 'Shipping on the Danube heading for the Levant and the Crimea is daily increasing. . . . Industry and manufactures are prospering in the absence of the prohibited goods. A large number of people from Nuremberg, Swabia and even from England, who used to make their living by producing in their own country, have recently settled here to carry on manufacture.'[6]

This economic development, which coincided with the agrarian reforms designed to reduce the degree of feudal exploitation and to turn the peasants wherever possible into hereditary copyholders, resulted in a rise in urban and rural living standards more marked than that occurring elsewhere in western and central Europe during this period. Of course, this rise was not general throughout the lands of the monarchy. Because of the difficulty of enforcing the government's policies in areas of unchallenged noble supremacy, such as Hungary,

Bohemia and Moravia, it affected chiefly the regions in which the population had been relatively well off previously, especially Upper and Lower Austria. There is much contemporary evidence testifying to the unusual degree of prosperity in these provinces. Caspar Riesbeck, a noted travel author, crossed the border from Bavaria in 1780, and was struck by the evidence of better cultivation and higher standards of living on the Austrian side of the border. Some of the peasants whom he saw driving to market seemed to him very much like the prosperous farmers of England or northern Holland. 'Everywhere,' he wrote, 'one sees evidence of well-being.'[7] The most obvious evidence of general well-being commented on by nearly all observers of the Austrian scene was the good quality and attractive style of the people's dress.[8] Travellers who, like Riesbeck, went on to Hungary, were once again forcibly struck by the contrast. Prince Esterházy's neighbours, Riesbeck wrote, looked like ghosts.[9]

66 Austrian peasants at leisure: drinking wine in the Brühl, Lower Austria.

Rising material standards coincided with the spread of education among all sections of the people. Maria Theresa laid the foundations for universal primary education in the 1770s, and under Joseph II primary schools were established on a massive scale in town and countryside.[10] Non-Catholics and Jews were admitted to all public educational institutions. As a result, cultural and recreational activities which in the past had been virtually monopolized by the nobility now brought different classes of society increasingly together. As always, this phenomenon shocked and alarmed conservatives. In 1778, Migazzi, the Archbishop of Vienna, lodged a complaint with the government against the ever closer contact between Christians and Jews. Among the records of the ensuing governmental deliberations we find the following outburst by a conservative member of the Council of State:

> It is evident . . . that young Jewish men, contrary to all custom, now go about in public dressed indistinguishably from Christians . . . some even with swords at their side. . . . They can be seen in public places in the company of young Christians. Likewise one sees Jewish women dressed in a manner little different from a lady of rank, walking in public in the company of Christian men and women. . . . Jewish people, indistinguishable from others by their dress, now frequent inns, ballrooms and theatres, and mix with the Christians who are there.[11]

Significantly, the enlightened Councillor Gebler managed to persuade Maria Theresa that the government could do little to alter this situation. The process of integration continued, and was of course accelerated by the legislation of Joseph II. It was specially noticeable in Vienna. In the Augarten and Prater, recently converted into public parks, the visitor could mix with a cross-section of the capital's entire population. Theatres were built in the suburbs to cater for the cultural appetite of their growing population. The Imperial collection of paintings was now open to the public in the Belvedere palace. On Monday,

67 The Lindenallee in the Augarten, which Joseph II opened to the public, and which, like the Prater, soon became a resort for all classes of the Viennese population.

which, in accordance with the time-honoured artisan tradition, was still a day of rest in Vienna, large crowds of citizens 'from the lower classes, artisans . . . and even humble servant girls with children in their arms' came to see the paintings.[12] In 1790 the University of Prague, for the first time, bestowed the degree of doctor of laws on a Jew.

68 'Popular
Entertainment', original
etching (1785), by
F. A. Maulbertsch,
intended for the growing
market for etchings which
resulted from the advance
of bourgeois culture.

69 The 'seller of etchings'
was one of the characters
in Johann Christian
Brand's *Kaufruf von Wien*
(1775), a work which was
itself a product of the
growing demand for this
form of art.

70 Performance of an opera by Haydn at the Esterhaz palace theatre, where the Baroque court culture survived for most of the eighteenth century.

THE EMERGENCE OF AUSTRIAN BOURGEOIS CULTURE

The power and privileges of the nobility and clergy had been seriously challenged by the reforms, which in turn raised the economic and cultural standards of all sections of the non-privileged classes. Naturally, the period in which this occurred also witnessed the erosion of the nobility's cultural hegemony and the assertion of the cultural and ethical values of the bourgeoisie.

Actually, the prolonged and serious crisis of the Habsburg monarchy which set in in 1733 produced a cultural *misère* for court and nobility which anticipated the bourgeois cultural offensive by nearly two decades, and created highly favourable conditions for its success. Financial difficulties compelled Maria Theresa soon after her accession to dismiss the splendid musicians who had been the glory of Habsburg court culture since the reign of Leopold I, and on whom Charles VI had been spending 200,000 florins a year. A mixture of financial problems and political demoralization prompted a reduction in the nobility's ostentatious spending. There was a sharp downward turn in building activity after 1740, and significant economies were made in expensive items such as funerals. When Count Gundaker Althann was buried in 1747 in conformity with a new simplified 'burial and mourning order', the court diarist Khevenhüller expressed the fear that it might not be possible to maintain noble supremacy in the long run without the traditional ostentation.[13] Significantly, the only family which continued the old cultural tradition on the grand scale was that of the Esterházys, who were among the greatest of the Hungarian magnates. The Hungarian aristocracy was not demoralized, nor were any of the major reforms applied to Hungary until 1785.

A new bourgeois culture could not develop from purely indigenous roots in Austria. Since the Counter-Reformation, the cultural life of the non-privileged classes had been almost entirely sponsored and organized by the church, and the church was far too closely linked with the court, the nobility and the *status quo* to be able to nurture a culture corresponding to the needs of a class which, consciously or otherwise, was in the process of creating a new society. The only surviving secular form of popular culture, the Viennese comedy, had degenerated into a mixture of elaborate mechanical gimmicks and vulgar buffoonery, as can be discerned even from Otto Rommel's apologetic analysis.[14] Just when it might have provided the starting point for a new national culture, it was desperately searching for ideas. The revival attempted and inspired by Philip Hafner came too late, and the comedy was therefore eclipsed for a time by rival cultural currents.

The first phase of the new culture in Austria was therefore bound to be an importation. A window was opened to the north, and Austria received the mid-eighteenth-century bourgeois culture of north Germany and Saxony. The main features of this culture, which incorporated significant English influences, are well known. It asserted the claims of the German language as a vehicle of literature and learning. It endeavoured to create a German lyric and epic poetry, and above all a German drama, which could stand comparison with the achievements of the French and English nations in these fields. It rejected the existing court culture, because it was French and Italian rather than German, and because its Baroque and Rococo forms and conventions seemed unnatural, frivolous, and sometimes downright immoral. It looked for alternative forms suitable for expressing the cherished ideals of naturalness, simplicity and genuine emotion, discerned these ideals in its conception of the art of ancient Greece, and so gave birth to the style of Neo-Classicism. It replaced traditional Christian dogmas and piety with 'natural religion', the core of which was an ethic of active virtue (*Tugend*) and an all-embracing love of men (*Menschenliebe*). Leibniz and Christian Wolff bequeathed to it the notion of a God perfect in human terms, who had created the world in the manner best suited to provide for the needs and enjoyment of his creatures. It was possible to feel at home in and take delight in such a world.

The earliest attempt to open channels of communication between the Habsburg monarchy and Germany were made in the late 1740s, when Joseph Freiherr von Petrasch founded a learned society in Olmütz, the capital of Moravia, and published a journal containing extracts from German publications. Neither the society nor the journal survived for very long. The next attempt, made in Vienna towards the end of the Seven Years' War, was more successful. A group of writers and scholars, including Joseph von Sonnenfels, founded the 'German Society', with the aim of popularizing the leading representatives of the new German culture – Gellert, Hagedorn, Rabener, Kleist,

Klopstock and others – and encouraging Austrian writers to take them as their models. Soon there appeared Austrian versions of the classic eighteenth-century medium for the diffusion of national culture, the cultural-moral weekly periodical. The first, *Die Welt*, was short-lived, but Sonnenfels's own *Der Mann Ohne Vorurteil* ('The Man without Prejudice') survived for three years and helped to transform the Austrian cultural scene. Michael Denis, a Jesuit who had begun to write German poetry at the beginning of the Seven Years' War, published the *Anthology of Shorter Poems of Recent German Poets*, which was Austria's first real introduction to the works of Klopstock and the poets of his and the previous generation.[15] The publication revealed the extent of the existing demand for the products of German culture, which was soon catered for by the enterprising publisher Johann Thomas Trattner, who printed cheap, attractive editions of these writers. The Austrian reading public turned from the legends of saints and books of pious edification to German literature and popularized scholarship (*anmutige Gelehrsamkeit*).

In the course of this cultural ferment, a controversy arose over the reform of the theatre. Sonnenfels and the protagonists of bourgeois culture sought to make room on the stage for a drama without the elaborate artificialities of the foreign plays presented at the court theatre, a 'natural' drama which would arouse the deeper human emotions, an original German drama, if possible. Their uncompromising refusal to accept the surviving Viennese popular comedy as a form of legitimate German drama was due to its generally low standards in the 1760s, but was also an expression of the moral prudery and social arrogance which is characteristic of so much bourgeois culture.[16]

Despite the controversy, it was in the field of drama that the new culture asserted itself most speedily and most successfully. Christoph Willibald von Gluck's well-known 'reform' of opera in the 1760s was clearly an attempt to adapt the conventions of music drama to the new cultural ideals. His sympathy

71 Joseph von Sonnenfels (1732–1817), the chief protagonist of bourgeois culture in Austria.

73 (above) Johann Michael Denis (1729–1800), the Jesuit poet who introduced the major German poets of the eighteenth century to the Austrian public, and who translated Ossian.

72 Johann Thomas Trattner, the successful printer and publisher, notorious for his numerous pirated editions of leading German authors.

119

for these ideals is revealed in his recently published correspondence, in which he refers to music which is 'simple and natural', which 'calls for enthusiasm', which is 'easy for a person who has feeling' and who can 'follow the dictates of the heart'.[17] In a preface to the opera *Alceste*, one of the first of the 'reform-operas' in which he collaborated with the librettist Calzabigi, he wrote:

> When I began to write the music for *Alceste*, I resolved to free it from all the abuses which have crept in either through ill-advised vanity on the part of the singers or through excessive complaisance on the part of composers, with the result that for some time Italian opera has been disfigured. . . . I sought to restrict the music to its true purpose of serving to give expression to the poetry and to strengthen the dramatic situations, without interrupting the action or hampering it with unnecessary and superfluous ornamentations. . . . I believed further that I should devote my greatest effort to seeking to achieve a noble simplicity; and I have avoided parading difficulties at the expense of clarity.[18]

Gluck's *Alceste* was the first production at the Vienna court theatre after the long closure which followed the death of Maria Theresa's husband Francis I in 1765. It was therefore the first to be reviewed in Sonnenfels's new periodical, *Briefe über die Wienerische Schaubühne* ('Letters on the Viennese Theatre'). He was enthusiastic:

> I am in the land of miracles. A serious opera without *castrati*, music without . . . gargling, an Italian libretto without bathos and frivolity. With this threefold miracle the Court theatre has been reopened. Indeed, I must add a fourth, and it is not perhaps the least: the principal singer is a born German. . . . The language of Mr Calzabigi is the simple language of genuine feeling; a stream which runs softly down a gentle slope, preserving its equanimity all the way, and getting aroused only when it bursts upon a stone lying in its way. . . . The music is by a man who not only manipulates chords and

harmonies, but who has discovered the accents of emotion, or if I might be allowed the phrase, the accents of the soul.[19]

Gluck's reform of opera was thus greeted as the first important step on the road to the new kind of drama envisaged by the protagonists of the new culture. The triumph of German over French drama at the Vienna court theatre followed surprisingly quickly. For in the struggle to defend its cherished French drama, the nobility found itself deserted by both Empress and Co-regent. With her fanatical concern for the moral standards of her court and capital, Maria Theresa felt the greatest anxiety about the roles played by the pretty French actresses off the stage. She firmly refused to contribute financially to the French theatre, and was much relieved when bankruptcy forced the French company of actors to leave for Italy in 1772. Joseph II was to some extent already under the influence of the new

74 Johanna Sacco, a popular actress and singer at the Vienna Nationaltheater.

75 Christoph Willibald von Gluck (1714–87), whose 'reform operas' represent an attempt to apply the Neo-Classical ideals of naturalness and simplicity to music drama.

culture. More important, however, than any personal inclination was his agreement with Sonnenfels and his allies that a reformed German drama could play an important moral and educative role in society. Such a role accorded admirably with his governmental objectives, and he threw the weight of his influence behind Sonnenfels and against Kaunitz, who fought a desperate rearguard action on behalf of the French company. In 1776, Joseph took the court theatre out of the hands of the impresarios, most of whom had bankrupted themselves, named it the Deutsches Nationaltheater and made it the permanent home of German drama. The German players henceforth received salaries from the state.[20]

It was a lucky coincidence that in Joseph II the Nationaltheater had an enthusiastic and competent theatre manager. He found, engaged and retained the loyalty of first-rate actors and singers.[21] Though an excessively cautious censorship sadly restricted the repertoire and prompted some unedifying adaptations, the Vienna theatre under the Emperor's management was acclaimed as the best German theatre of the time.[22] It acquainted the Austrian public with some of the works of Lessing and Goethe, after 1780 it introduced Shakespeare in the new German translations, and it encouraged the composition of dramatic works by Austrian authors, though few of these works have won lasting literary fame.

Despite the triumph of the German spoken drama, the permanent establishment of a German opera was not achieved in Joseph II's Nationaltheater.[23] For a time, the advocates of German opera, the most influential of whom was the actor-director J. H. F. Müller, won Joseph II to their side, and a German Nationalsingspiel was successfully inaugurated in 1778 with Paul Weidmann's comedy *Die Bergknappen* ('The Miners'), set to music by Ignaz Umlauf. Joseph was apparently pleased with the production, and seventeen German operas were produced during the following year. Soon after Mozart arrived in Vienna in 1781, he received a commission to compose a German opera which resulted in *Die Entführung aus dem Serail*. But the history

76 The Michaelerplatz, Vienna. On the right is the façade of the Nationaltheater.

of this work illustrates the growing opposition to German opera
by those who insisted on the maintenance of the traditional
monopoly of the Italian idiom in music. There was organized
hissing at the first two performances. As Mozart had taken great
trouble in the composition of this opera to fulfil all the criteria
of good music and drama insisted on by the protagonists of
German drama, it is inconceivable that the opposition could
have come from that quarter. Though the sources are not
explicit, it seems safe to assume that the nobility was expressing
its insatiable appetite for Italian musical fare. Joseph II's well-
known comment to Mozart about *Die Entführung* – 'too beautiful

for our ears and a tremendous lot of notes, my dear Mozart' – is ambiguous, but it does suggest that in this field Joseph was now prepared to yield to the taste of the nobility. Opera, after all, did not have the same educative function as spoken drama. Thus, after only five years, German opera disappeared from the stage of the Nationaltheater, and a company of Italian singers from Venice was engaged.[24] In the following years, the pure Italian style of Salieri, Paisiello and Soler y Martín achieved much greater popularity than Mozart among the court audience, whose hearts he managed to conquer only with his setting of the conventional *buffa* plot of *Così fan tutte*. Count Karl Zinzendorf, who had been bored by *Le nozze di Figaro*, found the music of *Così fan tutte* 'charming' and the subject 'rather amusing'.[25] Meanwhile, however, German opera re-emerged in the suburban theatres in the new form of a revived and reformed Viennese popular comedy, about which more will be said below.

Perhaps the most significant changes in musical culture were taking place outside the public theatre. In the days of flourishing Baroque court culture, music was written for great festive occasions. It was part of the formal entertainment which a sovereign or a great lord was expected to offer his guests from time to time. Now that the majority of noble families were no longer able or willing to spend on this scale, they clubbed together to organize 'subscription concerts' (*Akademien*) in the capital. On the subscribers' lists, the aristocratic names appear alongside those of the prosperous and cultured bourgeoisie. Moreover, in an increasingly bourgeois world, musical culture was now penetrating everyday life for the first time. It had certainly played no part in the everyday life of the Austrian nobility in the period of Baroque culture. Travellers visiting Vienna in the reign of Charles VI had found that the only social activity available in those noble houses which offered hospitality to guests and travellers, was playing cards.[26] In the 1770s and 1780s, many non-noble or recently ennobled families had become wealthy enough to entertain guests regularly in their homes. In these *salons* – not unlike the better known

77 A musical gathering in Vienna.

78 Wolfgang Amadeus Mozart (1756–91).

79 Announcement of the first performance of Mozart's *Die Entführung aus dem Serail*, 16 July 1782.

80 Ticket to a concert given by Mozart.

Parisian variety – the guest was not handed a pack of cards the moment he entered the door, but, to his pleasant surprise, was entertained with cultivated conversation and music. Women, who since the decline of the Renaissance had played practically no part in cultural life, now overshadowed the men both in the art of conversation and as amateur musicians (*Dilettanten*).[27] It was for the growing number of these amateur performers, with their great thirst for emotional stimulation, that C. P. E. Bach, Haydn and Mozart wrote some of their most inspired music. For the challenge to 'discover the accents of the soul', to use Sonnenfels's phrase, was the one that appealed most strongly to their own personalities and to their artistic aspirations.[28]

Judging from the evidence, the Viennese *salons* provided exquisite company and cultural stimulation of the highest order. Travellers and residents who frequented them have left glowing accounts.[29] Mozart and Haydn spent their happiest hours in these musical *Gesellschaften*, which constituted the public that they most cared about. After he had made contact with musical Vienna in 1781, Mozart could not face the prospect of returning to princely employment, and preferred to leave the security of the Archbishop of Salzburg's service. Haydn (who never permanently left the service of his slightly more accommodating employer, Prince Esterházy) nevertheless shared Mozart's feelings, and has left us a moving account of his emotions on leaving the *salon* of the Genzingers in the winter of 1790 to return to his routine duties at Esterhaz. After his arrival there, he wrote to Marianne Genzinger:

Well, here I sit in my wilderness; forsaken, like some poor orphan, almost without human society, melancholy, dwelling on the memory of past glorious days. Yes, past, alas! And who can tell when those happy hours may return – those charming meetings at which the whole circle has but one heart and one soul – all those delightful musical evenings that can only be remembered and not described? Where are all those inspired moments? All gone – and gone for ever. You must not be surprised, dear lady, that I have delayed writing to express my gratitude. I have found everything at home in confusion. . . . I slept little, and even my dreams persecuted me, for when I fell asleep and was under the pleasant illusion that I was listening to *Le nozze di Figaro*, the blustering north wind woke me and almost blew off my nightcap.[30]

The *salons* of Vienna had become the musical heart of Austria.

The picture may be rounded off by a reference to architecture. Despite the return of peace at the end of the Seven Years' War in 1763, and the subsequent economic development, there was, outside Hungary, no resumption of large-scale building activity by either the nobility or the church. Even in this field, in which the nobility and the church had made their most magnificent contribution to Austrian culture in the pre-Enlightenment period, the bourgeoisie was now coming to the fore. The only large town residence built during this period was that of the Swiss-born banker Johann Fries, who had made a fortune as court banker and as an army contractor during the wars, and who had since become a prominent manufacturer of cotton and brass goods. The peerage conferred on him by Joseph II in 1783 was regarded by the publicists as a welcome sign of the winds of change. In that year Fries commissioned Ferdinand von Hohenberg to build him a palace on the site of a dissolved monastery next to the Imperial Library. 'The architect has shown good taste,' wrote a contemporary observer, 'and has realized that in a building which can be seen as a whole, the simple is to be preferred to the over-ornate.'[31] Hohenberg had in fact built the first Neoclassical palace in Vienna.

The other important building erected in the centre of Vienna during this period was the Trattnerhof. The printer and publisher Johann Thomas Trattner, who had begun his career by issuing popular editions of the mid-eighteenth-century German poets, soon made a fortune in this period of an ever-growing reading public. Like Fries, he was ennobled, but unlike Fries he did not build a residence but a *Zinspalast* – a 'palace for letting'.

81 Detail of fresco by Maulbertsch in the theology lecture room of the new university building in Vienna. The subject is the Baptism of Christ.

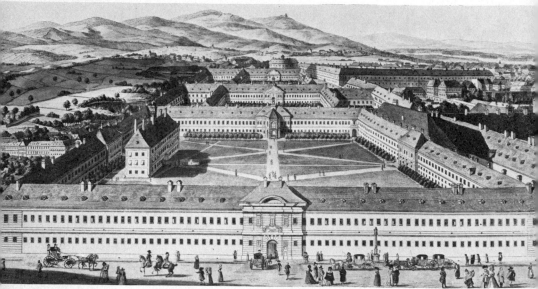

82 The General Hospital, Vienna, built in 1784.

83 The Academy of Military Surgery, Vienna, built in 1785; a successful blend of Neo-Classicism with the Austrian architectural tradition.

It was the largest house of its kind in Vienna, and yielded its owner 30,000 florins a year.[32]

Maria Theresa managed to complete the palace of Schönbrunn outside Vienna during the very first years of her reign. Subsequently, no more palaces were built on a grand scale by the Imperial family for the rest of the century. The Empress presented the reformed University of Vienna with a new building which was completed just before the outbreak of the Seven Years' War. It was built by the French architect Jadot in a sober French style, mediating, as it were, between Baroque and Classical elements.

During his reign, Joseph II commissioned two major buildings, whose purpose and style equally express the practical reforming priorities of the reign. The General Hospital was built in 1784. It is of enormous size, and its plain, uncompromising functionalism make it seem a modern building even today.

In the following year, a building was erected for the newly established academy of military surgery. In this superb building, the architect Canevale has successfully adapted Neoclassical forms to the Austrian architectural tradition. If there is a 'Josephinian' style in architecture, this building – the Josephinum – is its chief example.

The architecture of both the last-mentioned buildings demonstrates that under the influence of emerging bourgeois culture, the institution of monarchy was ceasing to rely on 'representation' and architectural symbols of its claims and power. A new university, a general hospital, an academy of military surgery – a monarchy which confined its architectural activity to buildings such as these, was evidently appealing to the new criterion of judgment: how much is it contributing to the general welfare? Judged by this criterion, how did the monarchy of Maria Theresa and Joseph II rank in the opinion of their own subjects?

THE JUDGMENT OF PUBLIC OPINION

The emergence of a body of public opinion on political affairs was both a by-product of the reforms and a natural consequence of the new bourgeois culture. In the period of confessional absolutism and noble supremacy, there was virtually no public opinion, because the ordinary people had been imbued with a doctrine of passive submission to 'God's will', and in any case they lacked the means whereby any opinions that they might have could be expressed. Thus, popular feeling on political affairs expressed itself only in times of exceptional strain or crisis in a rather elemental and immediate fashion. Food riots, outbursts of anti-Semitic violence, and the unflattering popular comment which followed the news of great military disasters, were the usual forms in which 'public opinion' was expressed during this earlier period.

When Maria Theresa embarked with determination on a programme of fiercely contested reforms, she had to meet the challenge of the opposition, who maintained that their legal rights were being violated. At first she evaded the challenge with the help of mere assertions, for example, that the rights claimed by the Estates were not rights but abuses, and that a more proportionate distribution of public burdens would be in conformity with a 'God-pleasing equality'.[33] But she could not get away with this for long. The opposition had chosen the weapons of political theory and history, and Maria Theresa had no choice but to fight them with the same weapons. Just as sovereigns engaging in inter-state conflicts had always needed the service of diplomats and political writers skilled in arguing their claim to a particular territory or jurisdiction, so a determined reforming sovereign like Maria Theresa needed civil servants and political writers who could present a *thèse royale* opposing clerical and aristocratic claims, and could act in accordance with it. It was precisely this need which prompted Maria Theresa to establish chairs of natural law in Austrian universities, for it was only with the aid of arguments drawn from natural law that some of the opposition's claims based on positive law and time-honoured practice could effectively be countered. It was the same need which prompted her, on the eve of the 1764 Hungarian Diet, to commission (with all due discretion) the publication of works like Kollár's treatise on the legislative powers of the kings of Hungary.[34] Similarly, in 1756 and 1769, when she was planning the large-scale suppression of monasteries, she commissioned books on the desirability of reducing both the number and the income of the monasteries.[35] These were arguments in which each side began with a premise which it was fully determined to maintain; there was no genuine dialogue. Each side was in fact appealing to some kind of public opinion for support. In any case, the arguments, which continued with mounting bitterness until 1792, and the political struggles underlying them, helped to arouse public opinion and to bring an increasingly large number of people into the controversy.

When, on the advice of Borié, a Councillor of State, Maria Theresa established the Chair of Administration and Commerce at the University of Vienna in 1763, and appointed Sonnenfels to it, her aim was to promote the social and economic reforms which the government was intending to undertake at the end of the Seven Years' War.[36] But the 'insolent' Sonnenfels, as conservatives called him, did not always keep to the government's brief, either in the lecture-room or as a writer. He was one of the first of those who drew practical political conclusions from the philosophy and culture of the Enlightenment. His weekly journal *Der Mann ohne Vorurteil* was the first of the German periodicals in which political and social issues were directly and sharply raised.[37] The criteria of his judgments were not Maria Theresa's actual legislative intentions, but her legislative obligations, which he believed he could deduce from the political theory of the Enlightenment and from the prevailing humanitarian ethics. In his writings and lectures he advocated the improvement of the condition of the peasants, which Maria Theresa intended to secure, the suppression of the guilds because of their restrictive practices, which was not in her programme, and drastic restrictions on the use of torture and on the imposition of the death penalty, both of which she was on the point of extending and aggravating in the notorious penal code of 1769. Indignant protests were addressed to the Empress, notably by the Court Chancellor, Chotek, and by Archbishop Migazzi. Chotek demanded that Sonnenfels be instructed to adapt his tenets to the existing laws. Migazzi complained because 'in all the writings of Sonnenfels the state is described not as it actually is, but as it should be according to his own fiery imagination.'[38]

Maria Theresa withstood the pressure for the moment, and assured Sonnenfels that he would be able to continue teaching in accordance with the principles which he considered right. But when he continued his campaign against torture and the death penalty even after the publication of the new penal code, the Empress yielded to his opponents, and ordered him to cease discussing these two issues. The protest which Sonnenfels submitted against this order is a tribute to his principles and to the courage with which he maintained them. Obedience to the laws

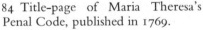

84 Title-page of Maria Theresa's Penal Code, published in 1769.

85 Methods of torture contained in the 1769 Penal Code.

as they stood, he argued, was not incompatible with criticism of their shortcomings. Without free criticism, improvement in the administration of the state was inconceivable. By offering such criticism, therefore, he was positively fulfilling the objectives of his appointment. He concluded his protest with a passionate and persuasive re-statement of his arguments against torture and the death penalty.

Though Maria Theresa reiterated her order, Sonnenfels's arguments, reinforced as they were at this time by the writings of Voltaire and Beccaria, had shaken her conviction. And only five years after the publication of the new penal code, so aptly named *Nemesis Theresiana*, she resolved that the question of torture be reconsidered. During the controversy which followed, Sonnenfels took a leaf out of the Habsburg book, and published the *votum* which he had submitted in his capacity as

133

Councillor of the Lower Austrian government, without openly appearing as the initiator of the publication. Maria Theresa, now thoroughly unsettled in her own views, asked her son, the Co-regent, to make the final decision without consulting her. At this decisive moment, Joseph hesitated and started another round of consultations, which proves that Sonnenfels was expressing his own independent views and not acting as Joseph's chosen mouthpiece. In the end, the *votum* of the Supreme Chancellor Blümegen provided the basis for Maria Theresa's formal decision that torture be abolished (1776). For the first time since the Reformation, public opinion had played an important part in the resolution of a political issue in Austria.[39]

The beginning of Joseph II's reign as sole Emperor marked the opening of a new phase in the history of Austrian public opinion. The majority of the clergy were fiercely opposed to his radical and comprehensive programme of church reform, especially to the Patent of Toleration and the suppression of the contemplative Orders. Some priests and bishops did not hesitate to express their opposition openly in sermons and pastoral letters.[40] In view of the strong influence still exercised by the clergy over the mass of the people in town and countryside, this represented a danger which Joseph could not ignore. To counter it, he relaxed the censorship regulations, so that supporters of his reforms could popularize them in cheap, easily readable publications. As in the previous period, the government was careful to avoid the impression of directly encouraging the supporters of the reforms to publish. Wittola, a leading Jansenist clergyman, and Watteroth, a Professor of History at the University of Vienna, wrote in defence of toleration. Numerous pamphlets on burials and other church ceremonies were published. The ideals of monasticism provided a favourite target for the sarcastic wit of the Austrian authors. None of them had any doubt that the powers which Joseph was asserting in ecclesiastical matters were of the very essence of sovereignty. When Pius VI announced his intention to come to Vienna in the spring of 1782 to stem the tide of reforms, it became necessary to ensure that

86 Pope Pius VI blessing the crowd from the balcony of the Kirche am Hof, Vienna, on Easter Sunday, 1782. ▶

the mass of the people did not harbour exaggerated ideas about the powers of the pope. Therefore, to quote the report of the British Ambassador, 'several Writers of Eminence and Ability have employed their Pens in representing to the Bulk of the Nation in short and cheap pamphlets the very narrow limits of the Papal Power in early Ages, and in proving that the gradual usurpation of the Roman Church in later times has been highly detrimental to the State and ought to be universally exploded.'[41]

Though the pamphleteering had begun under discreet government sponsorship, it subsequently developed and flourished spontaneously. For the majority of the intelligentsia and the journalists were enthusiastic, not to say delirious, supporters of the ecclesiastical reforms. A host of writers, and of those who wanted to establish themselves as writers, eagerly added their voice to the dawn-chorus of acclaim for the Emperor who was at last bringing Enlightenment to darkest Austria. There were interesting independent initiatives which enjoyed the good will and protection of Joseph and his ministerial supporters. A group of journalists, for instance, regularly attended sermons delivered in the capital and published a weekly commentary on them: the *Wöchentliche Wahrheiten für und über die Prediger in Wien*. This periodical lasted for two years and was followed by similar publications providing a wider coverage of church activities throughout the lands of the monarchy, and specializing in the exposure of non-compliance with government regulations. Leopold Alois Hoffmann, whose later anti-Jacobin publications achieved some notoriety, first made his name as a contributor to these periodicals.[42] The clergy were compelled to reply to this attack in kind, and they discovered one or two men in their own ranks capable of effective pamphleteering in the cause of tradition and orthodoxy. This of course made the controversy far more fascinating to the reading public. Sales of pamphlets increased, more writers tried to profit from the boom while it lasted, and the rising flood of publications became a source of astonishment to contemporaries.

Instead of attempting a serious study of this political literature, most historians have confined themselves to remarking upon its low intellectual quality and ephemeral character, implying more often than not that Joseph's subjects were not ready for freedom of the Press. They adduce statements by Joseph himself, which reveal his contempt for most of the publications, to justify their negative judgment. But Joseph has no claim to be regarded as an impartial authority on this question. Against his judgment may be set that of the writer Johann Pezzl, who said, 'Books educate scholars; pamphlets educate people.'[43] It may be argued that the word 'educate' here implies a subjective judgment. Nevertheless, Pezzl was calling attention to a fact which most historians have ignored – that the flood of pamphlets produced a new political consciousness among sections of the people which had hitherto been kept entirely outside the political sphere. The pamphlets were, as Sashegyi puts it, the Austrians' substitute for the political Press which was only slowly beginning to emerge at this time.[44]

The moment the political sphere was opened to the ordinary Austrian people, they – like Hanswurst on the stage of the Viennese comedy – claimed the right to have their say on what was happening. They discussed political questions at home, in the street, in coffee-houses and inns. It had all begun with an attempt to ensure popular understanding of, and acquiescence in, the ecclesiastical reforms. But once public interest was aroused, other issues were raised as well, both in pamphlets and in discussion. The British Ambassador referred to a freedom of debate which was 'almost as extensive as in England'.[45] As controversy continued into the later years of Joseph's reign, public opinion, as expressed in the political literature, became increasingly critical of his actions. Before analysing the reasons for this, I should like to say that I consider the emergence of this critical body of public opinion to be Joseph's most glorious achievement.

What, then, were the grounds of complaint? A careful study of the literature published in support of Joseph II's ecclesiastical legislation reveals that even this contained elements of criticism.

88, 89 The coffee house was often the scene of political discussions in Joseph II's Vienna: left, a pastel drawing of a Viennese waitress, 1744: right, bewigged waiter as a porcelain figurine of the period.

For many of his supporters, Joseph did not go far enough. Some pamphleteers called for the abolition of clerical celibacy (Pezzl dubbed it the crime of *lèse-nature*), and for the introduction of a completely German liturgy. Even the widely acclaimed Patent of Toleration left many supporters dissatisfied. The Emperor was careful to keep his policy within the limits of 'civil' toleration, and not to call into question the status of the Catholic church as the dominant church, maintaining an exclusive claim to the keys to eternal salvation. But the men of the Enlightenment had long since developed attitudes quite incompatible with such a status and such claims. They were men who had become uncertain about all traditional Christian teaching except the existence of a benevolent God and the Christian ethic. By the 1780s, some were even beginning to feel doubtful about the first of these beliefs. For these men the Patent of Toleration clearly fell far short of the requirements of justice. They asserted a man's right to profess any religious belief compatible with accepted morality, or to profess none. To them Joseph's persecution of the Bohemian Deists was an act of abominable tyranny. Thus, while Joseph's supporters in the ranks of the Catholic clergy tried to combat whatever survived of the old popular hatred of 'heretics', the Enlightened intelligentsia carried on a sustained campaign for the complete freedom and equality of all religions.[46]

The great strength of feeling behind the demand for religious freedom is well expressed in Alxinger's poem on toleration, which the poet was not allowed to include in the Austrian edition of his collected verse.[47] The most explicit criticism directed specifically against the limitations of Joseph II's toleration policy came from the pen of the novelist and playwright Franz Kratter:

> We only tolerate a few religious sects. While we give them the right to worship publicly, we forbid them churches which can be entered directly from the street and deprive their churches of spires and other symbols of dignity. We treat the

90 Franz Kratter (1758–1830), novelist and playwright, who advocated complete religious freedom and the participation of representatives of the people in legislation.
91 Johann Baptist von Alxinger (1755–97), whose poem on toleration (1784) was suppressed by the Austrian censorship.

Jews like strangers in their own fatherland. We confiscate the goods of the little band of Deists, and exile them to the Turkish border. We regard the poor fanatic who tries to win his fellow Christian for another denomination as a criminal, and treat him as such. And in our conversation every other word is toleration . . . toleration.[48]

The demand for religious freedom was frequently linked with that for complete freedom of the Press. Sonnenfels, while claiming the right to criticize existing and even recently enacted laws, never questioned the necessity of governmental censorship in defence of public morality. But in the 1780s, some writers expressed scepticism about the possibility that a completely free Press would cause any serious harm. Where freedom of the Press flourished, argued one author, the people learned to think. They thereby learned to protect themselves against anything harmful which a free Press might produce. The risks resulting from too little freedom of the Press far exceeded those resulting from too much: 'Rulers and ministers are likely to commit stupidities against which the writers might have warned them. It is of no great concern to a nation, whether or

92, 93 Two of the numerous pictorial expressions of support for the principle of religious toleration called forth by the 1781 Patent of Toleration.

94 Jewish salesman. An illustration from Johann Christian Brand's *Kaufruf von Wien*.

not some author spends his time writing stupidities. Such an author thereby does most harm to himself. But it is of very great concern to the nation whether or not a minister commits stupidities, because it is the nation which pays the price for them.' The anonymous writer concludes: 'Censorship is not only useless and unnecessary, but harmful. It could certainly be abolished without any damaging consequences. The nation should be given the freedom to sail upon the ocean of knowledge and opinion with the compass of its own powers of judgment, and to make new discoveries. Good sailing!'[49]

The critical accents which are barely discernible in the great chorus of praise during the early years of Joseph's reign are predominant in the publications which appeared after 1785. It is not, as has sometimes been assumed, that the writers were turning away from the premises of the Enlightenment. The reason for the increasingly critical attitude of the writers was Joseph's failure to live up to their standards of an Enlightened ruler. It might have been possible to forgive the half-heartedness of his ecclesiastical and censorship reforms. It was not possible to forgive his patent contempt for the profession of letters. Gottfried van Swieten, the bastion of Enlightened influence within Joseph's government, urged that authors' copyright should be protected by prohibiting pirated editions of their works. Joseph rejected the proposal for commercial reasons (1784).[50] He offered authors neither pensions, sinecures, nor honours. The long-standing project for the establishment of an Academy of Sciences in Vienna was not even seriously discussed during his reign. His care was almost exclusively devoted to the expansion of primary education. Joseph Richter was speaking for every writer when he complained: 'The best among our people desire that Emperor Joseph should show more respect for the arts and sciences, because it is humiliating for a nation, if its artists have to beg for their bread, and if the writers who have contributed to the enlightenment of the people are suffering deprivation. A people with our kind of constitution not only needs elementary knowledge; it needs the higher sciences and the fine arts.'[51]

97 The fate of convicts under Joseph II. Convicted prostitutes have their heads shaved and are sent to clean the streets. ▶

95 Title-page of Joseph Richter's pamphlet *Why is Emperor Joseph not loved by his people?* published by Wucherer.

96 Allegory on Joseph II's dissolution of the contemplative Orders, 1782.

Nowhere was Joseph II's policy more sharply and directly at variance with the attitudes derived from the philosophy of the Enlightenment than in his policy towards crime and punishment. So impatient was the Emperor to impose penalties which he considered more effective deterrents to crime than the death penalty, that he anticipated the publication of the new penal code, and commuted all death sentences imposed under the Theresian code. Enlightened opinion welcomed the abolition of the death penalty, but recoiled in horror at the sentences which Joseph substituted. For he substituted public humiliation and the slow martyrdom of hard labour for quick execution. The arbitrary character of this procedure, as well as the total lack of sympathy for the prevailing humanitarian ideas which it revealed, provoked a series of bitterly critical publications. Also, Joseph's practice of almost always increasing the sentences imposed by the courts was widely condemned as illegal.[52]

When the new penal code was finally published at the beginning of 1787, there was praise for its clarity and simplicity, but general condemnation for the cruelty of the punishments prescribed. Looking back after Joseph's death, Pezzl observed: 'The good sides of the penal code were recognized, and yet people objected to the frequent and almost universal prescription of the cane. This was rejected as an inappropriate punishment, likely to corrupt the character of a civilized people, and suitable only for barbarians and slave-minded peoples.'[53] The retention of the crime of *lèse-majesté*, which Joseph's brother Leopold, Grand Duke of Tuscany, had eliminated from the new Tuscan penal code, was noted with dismay. An Austrian correspondent drew attention in the pages of Schlözer's periodical *Staatsanzeigen* to the alarmingly wide definition of this crime: 'In chapter III, §43, this crime is said to be committed also by a person who "loses sight of the deference due to the sovereign, and insolently and publicly attacks him in speech or writing". . . . What does *attack* mean here? Is it intended that this crime should be imputed to someone who out of concern for the welfare of the state publishes his honest critical opinion about regulations issued in the name of the sovereign?' The correspondent went on to point out the generally harsh character of the code.[54]

Another subject which almost inevitably drew the fire of the political writers was Joseph's foreign policy. Under the growing influence of the Enlightenment, and especially since the Seven Years' War, more and more people discarded the traditional acceptance of war as a natural and permanent aspect of human relations. Rousseau's view of man as a normally peace-loving creature had asserted itself. It is the starting-point and basic assumption of the poet Alois Blumauer's *credo*: 'Two forces guide man wherever he goes: Nature gave him his understanding to think rightly; and to act rightly, it gave him his heart.'[55] Warfare was not, therefore, inherent in the nature of ordinary men. It was the result of the time-honoured but false statecraft which identified glory with pointless territorial expansion. If Joseph's aggressive alliance with Catherine II of Russia, and the resulting conflict with Turkey (1788–91), aroused dismay and indignation among the Austrian population, it was due to the prevalence of such ideas no less than to the material hardships which the war brought in its wake. 'What compensation is it to a grey-haired old father,' asked an anonymous pamphleteer in 1788, 'who has been robbed of his son, his joy, his all, that his sovereign has added ten kingdoms to his territories?'[56]

Once the fighting had commenced, there was naturally much patriotic talk and toasts were drunk to the destruction of the Turks. But in a play entitled *Die Kriegssteuer* ('The War Tax'), an anonymous author recorded such talking and toasting in the same spirit of burning indignation in which Karl Kraus was later to record the patriotic talk of the First World War. One must hope that the Austrian public read the play more carefully than the reviewer of the *Allgemeine Deutsche Bibliothek*, who was misled into believing that the author's aim was to promote a greater willingness to pay the 7 per cent war tax imposed at the end of 1788.[57] The leading characters of the play are a captured Turkish officer of great humanity and generosity, and a music-loving young lady whose favourite authors are Lessing and Shakespeare. The young lady cannot celebrate an Austrian victory without weeping for those who have lost their dear ones, while the Turkish officer makes a handsome sacrifice to ensure her happiness. In the final scene, the young lady's performance of Schubart's *Abschiedslied* arouses in the Turk and in the Austrian family a deep sense of their common humanity, and they all exclaim the words which are printed as a motto on the title-page: 'There is no salvation in war' (*nulla salus bello*). The young lady's uncle raises his hands, praying 'that all warring powers might heed this great truth', and the curtain falls. Considering that it was written in 1789, the year of Coburg's and Laudon's great triumphs against the Turks, the play is a most remarkable testimony to the strength of anti-war feeling in Austria.[58]

More significant than any criticism directed against particular policies was the opposition to absolutism itself, which became clear and explicit towards the end of Joseph II's reign. Though the supporters of Joseph's ecclesiastical policy were often content, when defending it, to invoke unlimited state powers in church matters,[59] the writers of the Austrian Enlightenment were not, on the whole, champions of absolute monarchy. For one thing, they craved for an assurance that the policies which they approved of would be continued by Joseph's successors. 'Trembling for the future', even in the balmy days of 1781, Watteroth pointed out the advantages of constitutional monarchy: 'Those states are more fortunate which have a Parliament not restricted to registering edicts but based on fundamental laws which protect the beneficent acts of their ruler against the arbitrary whims of future imbeciles, and facilitate all projects furthering the good of the state. In such states no Louis can easily revoke what a Henry has granted.'[60] 'Fundamental laws', spelling out how rulers must promote the general welfare and binding on them, were frequently advocated as the best guarantee against the danger of the succession of unenlightened rulers. Sonnenfels campaigned throughout his career for the promulgation of such fundamental laws, which would have bound future generations of Habsburg rulers to confine themselves to defending their subjects' security and promoting their livelihood.[61] The deliberate flouting of fundamental laws by the sovereign would have constituted a recognized crime against which the aggrieved subjects would have had legal remedies.

Quite apart from fears about the future, however, the feeling was expressed that the people should have a chance to participate in great reforms like those enacted by Joseph II. The welfare of the people was the proclaimed objective of these reforms, and the people, it was argued, had a useful contribution to make to the discussion of the requirements of their own welfare. The image projected by Joseph of a ruler promoting the general welfare, while disdaining opinion and circumventing representative institutions, did not seem to make sense. Most writers concerned with this problem thought that the existing provincial diets, reformed so as to include adequate burgher and peasant representation, could become appropriate organs for consultation and popular participation. Only Andreas Riedel, condemned in 1795 as a 'Jacobin', proposed a central parliament for the whole monarchy.[62] Before revolution had broken out in France in 1789, the doctrine of Natural Law that it was the sovereign's duty to promote the general welfare had developed in Austria into a doctrine of popular sovereignty exercised through representative institutions. For in a book published in that year, Franz Kratter asked all rulers to realize 'that despotism violates the purposes of creation and the sacred rights of humanity ... that when any important reforms are being considered, the nation is entitled to have its say; that it would be the most noble ... act of self-denial, if a sovereign of his own volition restricted the usurped powers of monarchial absolutism.'[63]

THE RISING OF THE SUN
The historian Gustav Gugitz, who knew the political literature of the Josephinian decade better than anyone else, has called it

the *Sturm und Drang* of Austrian literature.[64] This judgment seems entirely valid. While German drama of the *Sturm und Drang* period, with its psychological extremes and sensational suicides, was virtually banned from the Austrian stage, the intensity of feeling, and the revolutionary mood, which it reflected found direct political expression in Austria. German men of the Enlightenment liked to reprimand Catholic Austria for its tardiness in adopting Enlightened attitudes in matters of religion, but they were astonished by the sharpness of the political criticism in Austrian publications, because so many of them regarded uncritical adulation of Frederick II of Prussia as the height of political wisdom and radicalism.[65]

The criticism was so sharp, because it stemmed from a new outlook on God, man and society, an outlook which was far more radically unorthodox than that associated with the mid-eighteenth-century bourgeois culture which had permeated Austria in the 1760s. The diluted 'natural' Christianity inherited from England was challenged by a pantheism, derived from Spinoza, in which the sun was conceived of as the supreme embodiment of God and his attributes. Sun-worship, whether of the ancient Egyptian variety or purely imaginary, fascinated the mind and fired the imagination. In one of the many utopian novels of this period, in which the characters take off on a journey in space in a balloon, the following conversation takes place: '"So you worship the sun?" we asked. "Certainly," replied the old man. "Does not God's goodness radiate from it and God's all-providing beneficence, his greatness, splendour and majesty? Are there any more unmistakable and obvious signs of his divinity?"' A few pages further on, the inquirers witness an act of sun-worship in which the rising sun is greeted by a solemn hymn 'full of the most stirring emotion and simplicity', ringing out 'in the great, open temple of nature'.[66]

The desire to indulge the simple human emotions, which produced the sentimental novel and drama of the mid-eighteenth century, assumed in the *Sturm und Drang* generation a social and political dimension. The central theme of the sentimental novel and drama, the love between a man and a woman, was now placed in the context of the human love which ought to bind all men together. In the same way, the ethical ideal of virtuous action transcended the narrow family context to which it had been confined, and was applied to society and the relations between nations. Baffled by these wider concerns, the older generation was tempted to dismiss them as fashionable *Empfindelei* (sentimentality).[67]

The new horizons somewhat moderated the traditional optimism concerning the natural inclination of rulers to pursue the objectives set before them in the light of prevailing political notions. The *Sturm und Drang* generation tended to be sceptical about the ability of rulers, corrupted by their artificial upbringing and environment, to rise to the ethical heights required by the new humanitarian ideals. Nevertheless, nothing is more characteristic of the outlook of this generation than its glowing and impatient confidence that the dawn of the new era was breaking. The triumph of light over darkness, a notion inherent in traditional Christianity, but relegated by it to a transcendental, other-worldly sphere, was now boldly conceived of as not only possible, but impending in this world. The horizon was eagerly scanned for signs of the imminent sunrise. When the news that general primary education was to be provided in the lands of the Habsburg monarchy was conveyed in 1774 to Gottfried van Swieten, then Austrian Ambassador to the Prussian court, it elicited from him an outburst of almost millenarian enthusiasm: 'At last the time has come when the truth is emerging in new splendour from the dark clouds which have enveloped it, and is entering upon its rights.'[68]

The ground for this optimism was the prevailing belief that, despite the inevitable moral shortcomings of rulers, men could be effectively prompted to moral political action. Men's innate moral inclinations, the existence of which was the fundamental assumption of the *Sturm und Drang* generation, were believed to be capable of encouragement and development to the point where they would provide the springs for such action. What had to be done, above all, was to remove the existing religious and national prejudices, fostered by priests and princes respectively, which undermined and frustrated man's moral inclinations. An organized crusade against these prejudices, through the process of a comprehensive moral re-education, was therefore seen as the great task of the hour.

When Adam Weishaupt founded the Order of the Illuminati in Bavaria in 1776, he had this kind of objective before his eyes. The growth of this Order in the *Sturm und Drang* period provides a close analogy to the development of the moral theme in literature. Whereas pre-Illuminist Freemasonry had been no more than a kind of inner emigration, an oasis in which it was possible to escape from the prejudices and divisions of society at large, the Illuminati aspired to project their moral principles into society and thereby to transform it. At the end of the process there was the intoxicating vision of the universal brotherhood of man, transcending existing religious and

98 Certificate of membership of a Viennese Masonic lodge.

99 Meeting of a Masonic lodge in Vienna.

100 Unexpected visit of Joseph II to a Masonic meeting. The picture probably records an imaginary event.

national divisions, which has received its classical expression in the words of Schiller's 'Ode to Joy': *Seid umschlungen, Millionen!*[69]

In Austria, many Freemasons, especially the group led by the mineralogist Ignaz von Born, adopted the Illuminist outlook. A missionary order, dedicated to the crusade against prejudice and the moral education of humanity, and thereby ensuring the triumph of the sun and the light, became a common and popular theme in literature and on the stage. This theme increasingly preoccupied Mozart, and decisively influenced the development of his musical idiom. Already in 1773 he was enthusiastically at work composing choruses for Gebler's *Thamos, König in Ägypten* ('Thamos, King in Egypt'), a 'heroic drama' whose hero is the head of the Egyptian order of priests, widely regarded as the true ancestors of the Masonic order.[70] When at work on his first German opera, *Die Entführung aus dem Serail*, Mozart induced his librettist to transform the conventional plot provided for him, so that he could introduce the theme of overcoming national hatreds and assert the ideal of human reconciliation.[71] He wanted to follow this by composing an opera with this theme at its centre. The exclusion of German opera from the Nationaltheater frustrated this ambition for some years. In 1789, however, Mozart's friend and fellow-Mason Emanuel Schikaneder acquired the new surburban Freihaustheater and made it into a home of German opera. He collaborated with Mozart on an opera based on a dramatization of the Illuminist crusade, transposed, as in Gebler's *Thamos*, into the days of the Egyptian cult of Isis and Osiris. As the work was addressed to the audience of the suburban theatre, it had to be cast into the mould of the traditional Viennese popular comedy to which this audience remained obstinately attached and which experienced a revival in the new suburban theatres. It seems unlikely that Mozart felt this to be an irritating restriction. Despite its temporary degeneration in about the middle of the century, the Viennese popular comedy had nearly always been a vehicle for the expression of moral ideas. Casting his material into this form, with its obligatory magic entertainments and comic Hanswurst character, Mozart was able to express his ideals at a variety of levels, and to assert their universality.

The Magic Flute, which is still frequently misrepresented as a confused hotch-potch of incompatible ideas and elements, was in fact the most consistent and comprehensive dramatic expression of the political hopes, humanitarian ideals and educational aspirations of Illuminist Freemasonry. What seems to ill-informed commentators a nonsensical break in the plot, is in fact the process of truth emerging from the dark clouds enveloping it, which Gottfried van Swieten acclaimed in 1774, and which Mozart's generation hoped and believed to be taking place before their own eyes. Tamino and Papageno set out on their journey blinded by ignorance and prejudice. His first contact with one of Sarastro's priests makes Tamino realize that he has been stumbling in the darkness:

> *O ewige Nacht! wann wirst du schwinden?*
> *Wann wird das Licht mein Auge finden?*
> (Eternal night! When will you vanish?
> When will the light reach my eyes?)
> (Act I, Scene 15).

He agrees to submit to the rigorous course in moral education provided by the priests. Doubts expressed by a priest as to the ability of a prince to complete such a course successfully are allayed by a reminder that Tamino is more than a prince – he is a man (Act II, Scene 1). Papageno, too, is a man, and though he represents the traditional Hanswurst character, his role is by no means confined to providing comic relief in the solemn action. Though he fails some of the formal tests, he succeeds in the decisive one – for he has love in his heart, and it is the capacity to love which, even at a simple level, guides men in the direction of the light and brings them close to divinity (Act I, Scene 14). The prayer addressed by the priests to Isis and Osiris seems in its stirring simplicity to correspond closely to the hymn intoned to greet the rising sun in the novel referred to above, which was published a year before the first performance of *The Magic Flute*.[72]

We know how deeply Mozart was moved by all these ideas. 'If I go to the piano to sing something out of my opera,' he wrote to his wife when he was at work on *The Magic Flute*, 'I have to stop at once, for this stirs my emotions too deeply.'[73] We also know that these ideas met with an overwhelming response among Mozart's audience. Eva König, who was no admirer of Gebler's dramatic efforts, informed Lessing that *Thamos* was received in Vienna 'with the greatest applause'.[74] The dramatic critic Schink, who preferred Bretzner's conventional plot to Mozart's adaptation of it for *Die Entführung*, noted the contrary opinion of the Viennese public, who responded enthusiastically to Mozart's ideas. Disdainfully he recorded: 'One may count almost with certainty on a raging

101 Scene from Mozart's *The Magic Flute*. Papageno overcomes Monostatos with the aid of his magic bells.

102 Scene from *The Magic Flute*. The Three Ladies appear and deny Papageno's claim to have slain the snake.

success for a piece in which there is plenty of magnanimizing, bestowing, reconciling and forgiving, even if such results are arrived at in the most unnatural way.'[75] At the first performances of *The Magic Flute* Mozart was gratified to witness frequent applause and demands for encores, but he was delighted above all by the 'silent approval' indicating the deeper emotional response of his audience.[76] For two years after his death, *The Magic Flute* was the most frequently repeated production of the Freihaustheater.

In the light of this evidence about the ideas which inspired Mozart's work, and of the enthusiasm with which it was received by the general public, it is hardly too much to assert that *The Magic Flute* was the culmination of the Austrian achievement in the age of Enlightenment.

103 Joseph II taking leave of his ministers, shortly before his death.

104 Joseph II on his deathbed. ▶

IV FEAR OF REVOLUTION AND STAGNATION

When historians write about the tragedy of Joseph II's reign, they refer to his deathbed revocation of some of his important reforms in face of the formidable opposition of the nobility and clergy in Hungary, and to the humiliating reverses suffered by his armies. As Joseph was a wilful man, utterly convinced of the validity of his objectives, these events undoubtedly amounted to a great personal tragedy. However, the historical tragedy of the reign seems to me to lie at a deeper level. The tragedy for the lands of the Habsburg monarchy was that the character and limits of Joseph's objectives caused him to be concerned and dismayed at what may well seem to us today the most promising and positive aspects of Austria's development under his rule, namely, the vigorous intellectual life which his reforms helped to stimulate, and the emergence of a popular political consciousness.

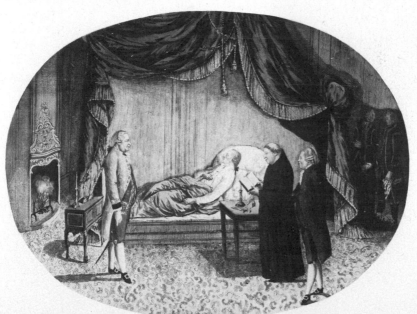

Until about 1786, Joseph confidently brushed aside all complaints and warnings uttered by Cardinal Migazzi that the changes in church-state relations and theological education were undermining the Catholic faith of his subjects. But in the course of that year he seems to have become concerned at the growth of unbelief, for he began to take steps designed to ensure that teachers kept within the bounds of Catholic doctrinal orthodoxy. Warnings to individual professors against whom complaints had been lodged by Migazzi were followed by a general warning to all 'not to teach anything which conflicts with the Catholic religion'.[1]

As long as Gottfried van Swieten remained at the head of the Commission for Education and Censorship, teachers who came under attack for their lack of orthodoxy had an influential protector within the ranks of the government. But by the end of his reign, Joseph II was clearly determined to remove van Swieten, if necessary, for the sake of reasserting Catholic orthodoxy in the schools and universities. A few days before his death, he addressed the following letter, evidently drafted by one of van Swieten's critics, to the Supreme Chancellor, Kollowrat: 'Since an essential aspect of the education of young people, namely religion and morality, is treated far too lightly, since the heart is not being educated and no feeling for one's true duties is being developed, the state is deprived of the essential advantage of having raised right-thinking and well-behaved citizens. Some months ago, these considerations led me to ask Councillor Heinke . . . for his frank opinion as to how the defects in the present educational system might be remedied.'[2] Kollowrat was instructed to consult Heinke with a view to submitting detailed proposals for educational reform. The instruction made it clear that van Swieten was to be excluded from educational policy-making in future. It is fascinating to speculate on what policies Joseph would have adopted to secure greater religious conformity and stricter moral standards in Austrian schools and universities if he had lived longer.

105 Gottfried van Swieten (1734–1803), President of the Commission for Education and Censorship, 1782–91. He fought a persistent rearguard action against the more repressive policies of Joseph II's later years.

An analogous trend can be detected in the censorship policy of Joseph II's last years. Here, too, Gottfried van Swieten, who was in charge of both education and censorship, interpreted his instructions in the broadest possible way, and permitted the publication of books reflecting his own pantheistic-humanitarian outlook. But from the end of 1783 onwards, Migazzi and the more conservative ministers occasionally succeeded in persuading Joseph to reverse van Swieten's decisions. In 1784, van Swieten's permission for the publication of the deistic *Glaubensbekenntnis aller Religionen* ('Faith Common to all Religions') was reversed after a conservative Councillor of State, Hatzfeld, had pointed out that love of nature's creator and of one's fellow men was commended in this book not as part of the Catholic way of life, but as the sufficient content of any true religion. After this decision, van Swieten was compelled to apply much stricter standards to the censorship of works dealing with religious questions, as Alxinger and the editors of the *Viennese Almanac of the Muses* (*Wiener Musenalmanach*) quickly discovered. Deistic works, radical biblical criticism of the kind so widely popularized at this time by Carl Friedrich Bahrdt, and all books throwing doubt on the validity of revealed religion, were now generally banned. The *empereur sacristain* was making it clear that after sweeping away the cobwebs of over-elaborate ceremonial and ancient prejudices, he intended the purified edifice of the Catholic faith to stand intact.[3]

When, at the beginning of his reign, Joseph II relaxed the censorship regulations in such a way as to allow freedom of political discussion, he assumed that this freedom would result in greater understanding of and support for his objectives. Political enlightenment, he thought, could only be conducive to the success of his policies. He gladly accepted the risk of the appearance of publications critical of himself, confident that such 'scurrilous libels' would be generally regarded with the contempt that he thought they deserved, and would ultimately enhance the reputation of a sovereign who felt sufficiently sure of himself to tolerate them. As late as 1787 (at a time, that is, when he was already seriously concerned at the attacks on the Catholic faith), he could not conceive that hostile political literature could represent a danger to his government or to his objectives. A resolution issued by Joseph in that year, relating to a highly critical pamphlet by Count Nicholas Forgách, the leader of the aristocratic opposition in Hungary, shows how lightly he still regarded the possibility of significant political opposition: 'This pamphlet is to be allowed to circulate freely, as have been all others which have concerned Myself alone and which have been much worse. . . . Count Forgách is not to be cautioned, because you cannot make a Moor white by washing him. If he should take matters too far, I shall know how to put him in his place.'[4] The Emperor thus dismissed political criticism as merely a personal attack on himself, and continued to think that the political situation was well under control.

106, 107 Flemish national hero and Joseph II as depicted in the *Brabant Chronicle* of 1790.

This confidence was shaken by the outbreak of revolution in the Austrian Netherlands. After the failure of the project to exchange the Netherlands for Bavaria in 1785, Joseph had lost no time in preparing the introduction of his administrative, judicial and ecclesiastical reforms into that province. Here, however, the opposition quickly went beyond the stage of formal protest and passive resistance, which Joseph had become accustomed to in the other provinces. For the clergy and the nobility, whose interests were directly affected by the reforms, enjoyed the enthusiastic support of the mass of the urban population. Mass demonstrations, rioting and armed rebellion throughout most of 1787, in which the disaffected students of the new General Seminary in Louvain played a leading part, compelled Joseph's Minister Plenipotentiary and the Governors to retract or postpone the measures which had been taken.

The link between the clerical and aristocratic initiators of opposition and the support of the urban masses was provided by a flood of inflammatory publications, some printed inside the province, others imported from the ecclesiastical principality of Liège. Joseph now realized for the first time how influential political publications could be, and that the authors whom he had so despised might be instrumental in frustrating his considered policies. And he reacted in characteristic fashion. In a letter to Trautmannsdorff, the new Minister Plenipotentiary, he wrote in December 1787: 'Scribblers [écrivailleurs] and publishers who indulge in libels must be severely punished. Those who oppose us with ridicule or threats must be arrested, whipped and kept in jail.'[5] This instruction resulted in numerous acts of oppression and persecution against booksellers during 1788, including a revival of the public burning of offending books by the hangman in the main square of Brussels.[6]

Joseph was not slow to apply the lesson which he learnt in the Netherlands to his other dominions. From the end of 1787 onwards, books containing critical comments on his policies and legislation were prohibited by the Censorship Commission on such grounds as that they 'undermined public respect for the government's policies', or that they 'described the administration of the state in a most repellent manner'.[7]

The proceedings against the publisher and bookseller Wucherer, who was something of a specialist in prohibited publications, illustrate the Emperor's changed attitude towards the question of the freedom of the Press. Wucherer had originally aroused the government's suspicion because of his connection with a new political secret society similar to the Illuminati – the Deutsche Union (German Union). But the discovery of his large trading stock of prohibited books prompted the Minister of Police, Count Pergen, to exceed his jurisdiction by urging on Joseph the adoption of stricter censorship regulations. He proposed that manuscripts should be allowed to be set up in print only after they had been passed by the censor, and that the sale of prohibited books abroad should be made a punish-

108 Johann Anton, Graf von Pergen (1725–1814), who in 1789 became the first Habsburg Minister of Police, and in this capacity tried to secure for the police immunity from all political and judicial control.

109 Georg Philipp Wucherer, the publisher who specialized in issuing cheap pamphlets critical of government policy, and in 1789 became one of Pergen's first victims.

able offence. The Minister of Police thus joined the Archbishop of Vienna in the campaign against van Swieten's Enlightened policies, and, as in the field of education, van Swieten could only mitigate, not prevent, the onset of reaction. As a result of his pleading, the scope of the new Censorship Patent of January 1790 was fairly precisely formulated, and the new penalties were confined to sellers of books 'calculated to undermine the principles of all religion, morality, and social order, and to dissolve the ties binding all states and all nations'. The Patent, however, unequivocally expressed Joseph II's recently adopted view that such books 'have a generally recognized dangerous influence', and that their suppression was therefore 'a duty towards humanity'.[8]

As a result of the dramatic developments culminating in the French Revolution, political comment was no longer confined to books and pamphlets, but could also be found in the newspapers whose numbers and readership were rapidly expanding.

Until this time, Joseph had regarded newspapers simply as a branch of the national industry to be fostered at the expense of foreign competition, and as a useful means of keeping his subjects informed of new laws and regulations, especially in the remoter regions of his monarchy. According to the official view, it was the job of the journalist to report news, not to comment upon it.[9] But Austrian journalists could not refrain from commenting upon the exciting events taking place in France in 1789. Moreover, as Ministers observed with mounting concern, these same events attracted many more people, 'even of the lowest class', into the ranks of the newspaper-reading public. According to police reports, even the plain factual reporting of these events gave rise to 'certain comparisons' and encouraged a 'rebellious mood' among this class of reader.[10]

Joseph's increasingly nervous government took steps, therefore, to control both the selection of news and political comment in newspapers. In July 1789, one Vienna newspaper was suspended 'because of the highly unsuitable selection of its news'. A few months later, Count Rottenhan, the Governor of Upper Austria, drew Pergen's attention to newspapers circulating in his province, in which 'acts of defiance by the mob of the authority of the sovereign, currently taking place in some countries as a result of an unbridled sense of freedom, are reported either without any adverse comment, or even in terms implicitly suggesting approbation'.[11] As a result, Pergen urged that he should be authorized to instruct all provincial governors to establish a regular system of censorship for the newspapers published in their respective capitals, in order to ensure the elimination of passages which might arouse 'wrong-headed conclusions, misunderstanding, or even a spirit of rebellion' among their lower-class readers. Joseph's simple *Placet* to Pergen's proposal, given a month before his death, was the signal for the establishment of a system of police censorship over all newspapers published in the lands of the Habsburg monarchy. Together with the Patent of January 1790 tightening up the censorship of books, it represented the legislative first-fruits of the newly established Ministry of Police under Count Pergen.[12]

The Ministry of Police, which exerted such a strong influence on policy at the end of Joseph II's reign, was itself a product of the Emperor's growing preoccupation with the state of public opinion and with the possibility of disaffection and rebellion which it seemed to indicate. The initiative for the establishment of the new ministry came from Pergen, who had entertained the ambition of becoming a Minister of Police from the time of his appointment as President of the Lower Austrian government in 1782.[13] It is not impossible that, as a result of Pergen's constant pressure, the ministry evolved more quickly than it might otherwise have done. This would explain why, as early as 1786, when Joseph was extremely confident of the strength of his position and of the prospects of his reign, he sanctioned a 'Secret Instruction', drafted by Pergen, which added to the manifold 'public' responsibilities of the police the 'secret' task of observing 'what people are saying about the monarch and his government, what the general attitude of the people is concerning the government, whether there are any malcontents, or even agitators, at work among the upper or lower classes, all of which is to be regularly reported to headquarters'.[14]

Whatever significance we may attach to the 'Secret Instruction' of 1786, it was undoubtedly Joseph's subsequent anxiety about the growing political disaffection of his subjects, and about the threat of open rebellion in a number of provinces, which led him in 1789 to agree to Pergen's importunate demand that the police organization throughout the lands of the monarchy be 'hived off' from the provincial administrations and be centralized under his own exclusive control. Pergen made an absolute fetish of secrecy, and insisted on the complete autonomy of his ministry within the government as an essential prerequisite of the effectiveness of the secret police. It is symptomatic of his growing influence over Joseph that the Emperor dealt with all questions concerning the police in his cabinet, without consulting the Council of State. It was also due to

Pergen's influence that the only information of the change given to the general public was a brief announcement that the Vienna police organization had been raised to the status of a ministry (*Hofstelle*).

After the organization of the police had been centralized under Pergen's authority, the observation of public opinion overshadowed all the other tasks of the police. The report, submitted to the Emperor every week, on the people's mood and opinions (*Stimmungsbericht*) was now the most important part of the work of every provincial director of police. Haunted by the multiplying symptoms of disaffection and rebellion, Joseph allowed Pergen to introduce all the worst features of a police state into the Habsburg monarchy: the recruitment of police spies from all classes of the population, the use of *agents provocateurs*, indefinite police detention of suspects without trial, and the arbitrary persecution of persons considered politically 'dangerous'.[15]

The employment of the entire range of police state security tactics did not, however, succeed in preventing the outbreak of rebellion in Hungary and Tirol, where Joseph's policies had created a revolutionary situation. It did succeed in seriously restricting the great uninhibited political debate in Vienna – a debate which, as we have seen, Joseph himself had stimulated, but which he now deplored as he embarked on his struggle against the onset of revolution. In the second instalment of the *Skizze von Wien*, published in 1789, Pezzl described Vienna as a city in which complete freedom of speech still prevailed. In the sixth instalment, published in 1790, he painted a very different picture. In the *salons*, the relaxed, uninhibited freedom of speech had disappeared. Political topics were avoided in conversation; everyone knew that walls had ears.[16]

MAINTAINING THE IMPETUS OF REFORM – LEOPOLD II

At no stage of his reign was Joseph II deterred from the pursuit of his basic objectives either by the occurrence of rebellion, or by concern at the development of public opinion. When his

110, 111 The revolt of the Wallachian peasants in 1784. Left, Horia and Gloska at the head of the insurgents; above, another rebel leader, Grisan Giorg.

first measures in preparation for the extension of the reforms to Hungary resulted in the violent *jacquerie* of the Rumanian peasants led by Horia at the end of 1784, the further changes planned were not even delayed, let alone abandoned. Similarly, Joseph's concern at the direction which public opinion was taking towards the end of his reign in no way weakened his determination to continue the programme of reforms. Apart from education and censorship, none of his policies were affected by second thoughts in this last period of his reign. When he revoked all but three of his Hungarian reforms in January 1790 in face of the growing opposition led by the nobility, he did not intend that these reforms should necessarily be abandoned for good. Joseph hoped that the sweeping character of his concessions, which went beyond the necessities of the situation at the time, would have the result of weakening the demand for an imminent meeting of the Hungarian diet. By

167

postponing the meeting of the diet indefinitely, or at least until some calm had been restored, he hoped to keep the door open for a resumption of reform.[17]

Nevertheless, Joseph's later policies did adversely affect the prospect of reform. For Pergen's elevation to the status of Minister of Police brought powerful reinforcement to the already extremely obstinate ministerial opposition to the reforms. Pergen, in fact, quickly became the principal spokesman of this opposition. His influence on some aspects of policy had become so considerable by the end of 1789 that he felt in a sufficiently strong position to offer the Emperor advice on a whole range of questions quite outside the jurisdiction of his department. In his Note of 16 December 1789, he advocated a conciliatory message to the Hungarian Estates, and came very near to submitting a complete draft of such a message.[18] The gracious terms in which the harassed Emperor replied to this Note encouraged Pergen to offer his services quite explicitly as general adviser on policy: 'Your Majesty has received my remarks on the threatened rebellion in Hungary so graciously that I am encouraged thereby to submit to Your Majesty from time to time my opinion on all aspects of Your Majesty's government.'[19]

As the Emperor once again replied in gracious terms, Pergen now set to work on a long and comprehensive indictment of Joseph II's reform programme. It was extremely outspoken, though prudently cast in the form of a police report on the political comments made by members of the 'reasonable public'. In the name of this public, Pergen upbraided Joseph for ignoring the advice of his senior Ministers and the protests of the Estates, for devising a tax system which was the ruin of the nobility, and for sanctioning a civil and penal code which all but abolished the distinction between the nobility and the lower orders. He pointed to the infringement of the property rights of the nobility and the clergy as the principal cause of unrest even in the non-Hungarian provinces, and in the light of this reading of the situation urged the repeal of the February Patent on the land tax and labour services, enclosing, for good measure, a draft patent of repeal.[20]

Soon after this was written, Joseph's deteriorating health compelled him to abandon the day-to-day control of the administration, and to re-activate the defunct Conference of State (*Staatskonferenz*) under the presidency of Kaunitz. That is why Pergen took the trouble to send Kaunitz a copy of the report that he had submitted to Joseph. The Chancellor of State had been one of the principal initiators of the administrative and ecclesiastical reforms, but in 1787 he had strongly counselled concessions to the opposition in the Netherlands. By the end of 1789, he was so alarmed by the developing crisis, especially in Hungary, and by Joseph's tardiness in making concessions, that he was prepared to collaborate with Pergen in a *démarche* designed to impose a policy of far-reaching concession on the ailing Emperor. Joseph was now too weak to resist such pressure, and the revocation of many of his Hungarian reforms had become an inescapable necessity.

When Leopold of Tuscany arrived in Vienna in March 1790, nearly a month after his elder brother's death, Belgium and Hungary were in open rebellion, the Estates in the other provinces were seizing the initiative and assembling unofficially, and the senior Ministers were urging upon Leopold wholesale concessions to the privileged orders. Kaunitz, moreover, the initiator of so many reforms under Maria Theresa and Joseph, now warned Leopold against further reforms for the time being, 'because they usually result in the confusion and dislocation of the administration'.[21]

In this situation, Leopold obviously had little choice but to acquiesce in the initiative taken by the Estates, and to follow the unanimous advice of the senior Ministers. Accordingly, he officially convoked the diets in all his provinces, abolished the General Seminaries as a concession to the bishops, and repealed the February Patent on the land-tax and the commutation of labour services as a concession to the nobility. For the time being, Leopold also gave a free hand to the ministers to continue and develop the repressive policies for the control of public opinion which they had been successfully urging on Joseph II since 1787.[22] To all appearances, the new reign inaugurated an era of reaction and repression.

Appearances, however, were in this case misleading. For Leopold, who proudly looked back on a quarter of a century of largely successful reforms in Tuscany,[23] was no less determined than Joseph had been to continue the work of reform in the lands of the Habsburg monarchy. But he wanted to avoid what he regarded as the mistakes which his brother had made and which had led to the monarchy's crisis. These mistakes, he thought, lay not in the ends but in the means. Two features, therefore, distinguish Leopold's reforming activity from that of his brother. Firstly, knowing from the latter's as well as from his own experience that a ruler who has simultaneously aroused the hostility of all sections of the population is powerless, he took great pains to win and retain the support of the non-privileged classes. Secondly, knowing from the examples of the American and French Revolutions that attachment to constitutional government was not confined to the privileged classes, but was an increasingly important aspect of the new popular political consciousness, he tried to act constitutionally through the revived representative institutions to which he admitted, or prepared the ground for admitting, an increased number of representatives of the burghers and peasants.

In his attempt to win the support of the non-privileged classes, Leopold made much greater use of the printed word than his predecessors had ever done. Whereas Maria Theresa and Joseph II had occasionally commissioned a scholar to put the government's case on a particular controversial issue, Leopold employed a whole swarm of journalists and others to 'sell' himself and his policies to the reading public. Publications directly (though of course secretly) sponsored by him ranged from an account of his reforms in Tuscany to polemical attacks on the demands of the privileged orders, especially in Hungary.[24]

It is difficult to assess how effective this propaganda was, or how faithfully the propagandists reflected Leopold's own ideas; on this question there were indeed some unedifying disputes between them. By itself, the propaganda could not have achieved much. The legislation of the National Assembly in France was already raising the expectations of the non-privileged classes outside France. What mattered, therefore, was the extent to which Leopold's propaganda reflected his government's practice, that is, the extent to which his policies corresponded to the aspirations and interests of the non-privileged classes.

If we examine the legislation which followed the first concessions to the privileged classes, we do in fact find that Leopold modified those of his brother's policies which had been most generally criticized in the political literature. He won the applause of the literary world for his willingness to concede authors' claims for some copyright in their works.[25] He eliminated the worst barbarities of the Josephinian Penal Code, which had been so loudly and universally condemned. The conclusion of hostilities against the Turks (marked by the Congress of Sistova in 1791) was greeted with as much relief and rejoicing as one would have expected in view of the dismay which had been provoked by their commencement under Joseph, although the yielding of Belgrade, conquered by Laudon in 1789, was deplored.[26]

Perhaps the most remarkable of Leopold's modifications of Josephinian policy, however, was his establishment of legal controls to circumscribe the arbitrary activities of Pergen's Ministry of Police. The ministry's proceedings against the publisher Wucherer and others were made the subject of investigation by the Supreme Judiciary. Pergen protested against this breach of his principle of secrecy, which Joseph had consistently respected. The Supreme Judiciary submitted a sharply critical report, on the basis of which Leopold reprimanded Pergen's ministry for its illegal proceedings and issued specific regulations governing arrests and investigations by the

112 The meeting between Leopold II and Frederick William II of Prussia at Pillnitz, 1791.

police, regulations which were closely modelled on the English principle of *Habeas Corpus*. He accepted Pergen's resignation (February 1791) and entrusted the reorganization of the police to Sonnenfels, Pergen's principal critic.

The new police organization was based on an amalgamation of Sonnenfels's constitutional principles and Tuscan precedents. The emphasis was put overwhelmingly on the public functions of the police, which were expanded by the attachment of a rudimentary public health service to the police administration. In accordance with Sonnenfels's belief that the citizen had the right to be informed of the organization and powers of the public authorities, the decree published on 1 November 1791, announcing the establishment of the new police organization, was the size of a booklet. It was, indeed, almost indistinguishable from the official instructions issued to the police personnel. The

113 Kufstein, the fortress in which most of the political prisoners were held during the 1790s.

records show that under the new system the police force became much more efficient in the performance of its public functions, and that the poorer sections of the Viennese population made extensive use of the public health service. On the other hand, the task of reporting on the political mood of the public receded into the background. It was not that Leopold was not interested in this kind of information; but he preferred to obtain it from a network of confidential agents working under his personal control.[27]

One action threatened to lose Leopold the support which he was so assiduously canvassing: his participation, with the King of Prussia, in the Declaration of Pillnitz (August 1791). The declaration, though making intervention against revolutionary France conditional on the concurrence of all the great powers, was believed to herald a war and therefore provoked an almost

173

unprecedented storm of public criticism. When reports of this criticism reached him, Leopold at first reacted with an outburst of indignation and with threats, in a manner strongly reminiscent of Joseph.[28] Subsequently, however, he was at great pains to modify the impression left by the declaration. He adopted a policy of studiously avoiding any worsening of his relations with France, countering all the efforts of the French *emigré* nobles to provoke war. Edmund Burke, who was running a campaign for an armed crusade of all Europe against France, could at this time find no words to 'express the folly and perfidy of [Leopold's] proceeding'.[29] But Leopold regained the confidence of his subjects, most of whom, as the British *Chargé d'Affaires* in Vienna observed, entertained great doubts of the expediency of a war against France.[30]

Leopold's reform of the Estates, to make them more widely representative, served a double purpose. Like the measures just referred to, it was bound to help him win support among the non-privileged classes in whose interest the reform was undertaken. It also directly weakened the offensive power of the privileged orders, because the Estates ceased to be the automatic and unanimous organs for the expression of their aspirations. The reform of the Estates was remarkable above all for the public agitation which accompanied it. The exclusive and reactionary demands put forward by the privileged orders to the Commission on Grievances provoked the non-privileged into taking political action on their own behalf. In Styria, a highly organized campaign was mounted by the inhabitants of the towns to secure representation on the Styrian delegation to the Commission on Grievances and in the Styrian diet. When the campaign ended in success (May 1791), the peasants followed the example of the towns, and petitions were taken from village to village for the collection of signatures. Leopold welcomed and even encouraged such initiatives, so much so that in Hungary, where the burghers and peasants were too demoralized and oppressed to initiate political activity, he instructed his own confidential agents to organize the campaign for the representation of these classes in the Hungarian diet.[31]

Just as Leopold II subtly exploited the conflict of interest and outlook between the privileged and non-privileged classes of society, he also tried to encourage the initiative of the middle and lower ranks of the bureacracy, among whom there was still considerable enthusiasm for the reforms, as a means of neutralizing the obstruction to be expected from the senior Ministers, all of whom had made their objection to further reform abundantly clear. To this end, a series of administrative directives issued at the end of 1791 established various forms of direct contact between the Emperor and his civil servants, extended the competence of departmental councillors at the expense of the Ministers presiding over departments, and provided new channels through which Leopold would be able to exercise personal control over the administration.[32]

Leopold's unexpected and early death on 1 March 1792 presents the historian with questions to which no definitive answer will ever be possible. However, I would venture the assertion that we can make sense of the intensive activity which filled the two years of his rule over the Habsburg monarchy only if we assume that he intended to maintain and extend the great programme of reforms initiated by his mother, albeit in the careful and subtle manner which the crisis provoked by Joseph's continuation of it had made absolutely imperative. The earlier view of Leopold's reign as the beginning of the period of repression and reaction is no longer tenable in the light of the evidence now available. We cannot of course say precisely what further reforms he intended to adopt. There is much evidence indicating that at the time of his death he was on the point of enforcing commutation of labour services on all private demesnes, his repeated demands to the Estates to submit their own proposals to this effect having produced no result.[33] This would have brought the more important part of the repealed February Patent into effect, though we may assume that Leopold would have tolerated a greater degree of variation from province to province than his brother. Another agrarian reform which

175

Leopold prepared was the leasing of all the secularized Jesuit and monastic lands to peasants, individually or collectively, in hereditary tenure.[34] There is also some fragmentary evidence indicating that Leopold was holding fast to the Josephinian land survey as the future basis of the land-tax.[35] For the rest, we can only speculate.

Would Leopold II have been more successful than Joseph II in overcoming the opposition which the continuation of the reform programme would inevitably have aroused? The basis of support among the non-privileged classes which he tried to create, and the co-operation of public opinion and representative institutions in the reforms which he tried to secure, would certainly have put him in a stronger position to face the opposition than the position to which Joseph was confined by his absolutism. His administrative preparations might have provided a more promising formula for overcoming the obstruction of Ministers than Joseph's intemperate sarcasm and self-righteous outbursts. If there was any chance of ultimately avoiding war with revolutionary France, Leopold – as Burke clearly saw – would not have missed it, and the work of reform would not have been undermined, as was Joseph's, by a foreign policy incompatible with its successful pursuit. Once again, we are in the realm of speculation: given a few more years, the reign of Leopold II might have been the culmination of the Habsburg achievement in the age of Enlightenment – the culmination, indeed, of Enlightened Absolutism.

THE END OF REFORM – WAR AGAINST FRANCE – STAGNATION
The problems presented by Leopold's reign are sometimes ascribed to his enigmatic and devious character. Perhaps they may more appropriately be seen as an illustration of how difficult it had become by 1792 to maintain and develop a programme of radical reforms. It required the ability to play off antagonistic social groups against each other, and the self-confidence to act against the inclinations of all the senior Ministers and to rely instead on the co-operation of men 'raised from the dust'.

Leopold's eldest son, Francis II, was endowed with neither this ability nor this self-confidence. His almost naïve straight-forwardness made it difficult for him to co-operate in the subtle, underhand preparations for his father's intended reforms, which Francis quickly wound up after his accession. Reluctant to rely on his own judgment, he promoted his former tutor, Count Francis Colloredo, to the position of Cabinet Minister, and generally deferred to his advice, as well as to that of his senior Ministers, Kollowrat, Hatzfeld and Pálffy. These veteran opponents of reform were now also suffering from the shock which the upheaval in France had inflicted upon them, and were pressing for the restoration of the declining influence and prestige of the clergy and the nobility as a bulwark against revolution. Francis's deference to the advice of these men led to the almost immediate lapsing or abandonment of all Leopold's projects for reform.[36]

If Francis had also been inclined to defer to the advice of Kaunitz, he might at least have postponed or avoided a war with revolutionary France. But Kaunitz had ceased to maintain direct contact with his sovereign since Joseph II's fatal illness, and his deputies, Anton von Spielmann and Count Philipp Cobenzl, exploited Francis's inexperience in order to launch an independent policy of their own which they hoped would bring them more prestige than they were ever likely to acquire as the obedient executants of their chief's policy of caution and restraint. In league with the emissaries of Frederick William II of Prussia, they presented the prospect of a war of intervention against the French Revolution as an opportunity for the new Emperor to begin his reign gloriously as a *propagator Imperii*, perhaps even to accomplish the design whose achievement had eluded his uncle – the acquisition of Bavaria in exchange for the distant Netherlands. When Kaunitz discovered the nature of the Austro-Prussian negotiations, he asked to be relieved of the office which he had held continuously for forty years. Francis allowed him to resign. Guided by Spielmann and Cobenzl, he adopted a foreign policy which, in the event, imposed on Austria the main burden of the campaigns against France, while only Prussia and Russia were rewarded with territorial acquisitions at the Second Partition of Poland (January 1793).[37]

As his country had not yet had a chance of recovering from the strain of the Turkish War, Francis was obliged to refrain from financing his new war by means of a war tax. He thus found himself helplessly dependent on voluntary financial support. Patriotic collections organized by humble loyalists could not disguise the fact that only large subsidies voted by the Estates could meet the requirements of the situation. The earlier abandonment of Leopold's projected reforms was therefore quickly followed by further concessions exacted as the price for the subsidies voted by the Estates of Belgium and Hungary. There were further concessions to the church, too, which may have been intended as the price for its moral support. The most notable of these was the dissolution of the Commission for Ecclesiastical Affairs under Kressl (November 1792). This was the first concession to the church comparable in significance to the concessions which had already been made to the nobility. The dissolution of this department also gave Francis the opportunity of carrying out a general reorganization of the central administration. When this was completed, most of the known supporters of reform, including Kressl himself, found themselves in compulsory retirement. Francis, to quote his own words, had 'cleared out all the black sheep'. Any resumption of a reforming policy was now out of the question in the foreseeable future. The administrative reorganization and the purge of November 1792 mark the end of the period of reform which had been inaugurated by the administrative reorganization of 1749.[38]

At a time of developing political consciousness, there was bound to be considerable resentment at so sudden a change in the political outlook. Once again, as at the end of Joseph II's reign, we can discern the symptoms of political disaffection among the non-privileged classes. There was widespread unrest in the villages, especially in Bohemia, as the peasants realized

114 Loyal citizens making voluntary contributions to help finance the war against revolutionary France in 1793.

that they were to be constrained to continue rendering labour services and paying tithes, with no prospect of commutation except by mutual voluntary agreement, which could rarely be reached. A mass of leaflets, urging resistance to the lords, circulated in Bohemia; one of these purported to have been issued by 'the [so far] secret National Convention of free Josephinian Bohemia in Prague', evidence both of the enduring popularity in the villages of Joseph II's agrarian reforms, and of the continued influence exerted by developments in France.[39]

Disaffection among the intelligentsia mainly took the form of indignation at the war with France. Quite apart from the financial burdens which it entailed, the war was opposed on political grounds. Austrian adherents of the Enlightenment saw in the French Revolution, for all its violent episodes, an attempt at the realization of their own political ideals. The similarities between some of the legislation of the French National Assembly and some of the reforms of Joseph II did not escape them. The Abbé Strattmann, a friend and colleague of Gottfried van Swieten, expressed his opinion of the French Revolution as follows: 'I liked certain aspects of the French Constitution of 1789 . . . because I am of the opinion that it actually exists in our monarchy, and that it is almost entirely worked out in accordance with the principles taught in our universities . . . for some considerable time.' A Styrian town clerk, speaking for those who had organized the campaign for better town representation in the diet, expressed a similar view: 'We agreed with the first French Constitution, because we thought that it would further the welfare of France, and because we found that it contained several provisions which the Emperor Joseph had introduced into the states of Austria. I mean the dissolution of the monasteries, the abolition of serfdom, the new system of taxation, and similar measures.'[40] Unlike Francis and his advisers, the intellectuals realized that a war of intervention against the French Revolution could not be quickly and successfully concluded, since armies could not be effective against a whole people.

The disaffection among the non-privileged classes was probably more intense and widespread now than it had been at the end of Joseph II's reign. But as the privileged classes were now largely reconciled to the monarchy, the unrest was less important, and by no stretch of the imagination could it be regarded as a serious danger to the state. There was, however, an additional factor in the situation which explains the extreme nervousness displayed by Francis and his ministers in face of this disaffection. That factor was the catastrophic failure of the government's foreign policy. There was an obvious connection between the rhythms of external and internal developments. Whenever the war against France went badly and other humiliations were inflicted on the Habsburg monarchy, the government adopted a policy of rigorous internal repression. The failure of the campaign of 1792, ending in the French

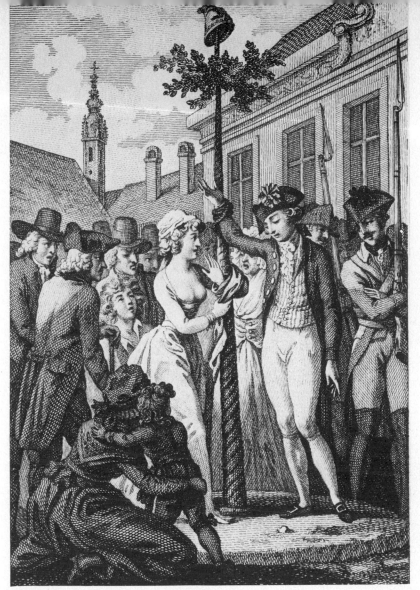

115 The 'tree of liberty', complete with 'Jacobin cap', the main symbols of support for the French Revolution.

invasion of Belgium and the Rhineland, and the humiliation of the Second Partition of Poland, were followed by the re-establishment of the autonomous Ministry of Police and the recall of Pergen from the retirement into which Leopold's policy had forced him. Once again, the police had to concentrate on observing and reporting on the political mood of the people. Nothing, according to Pergen's new instructions, was to be regarded as too trivial to be reported. The health service, which had been established in the course of Leopold's reforms of the police, was drastically cut to provide more time for 'secret police' activities. Pergen would have abolished it altogether, had he not been convinced that such a course would have produced serious unrest.[41]

The more serious and dramatic Austrian reverses of 1794, culminating in the defeat at Fleurus and the final loss of Belgium, which were accompanied by revolution in the remnant of Poland and rumours of Jacobin conspiracies in various other parts of Europe, roused Pergen and his new deputy, Count Saurau, to activity of feverish intensity. They now considered it imperative to arrest and silence the most persistent and outspoken critics of government policy, many of them Freemasons and Illuminati and some of them former confidential agents of Leopold II, who had been encouraged by recent events to discuss possible ways of organizing themselves for the more effective dissemination of their views. Chafing under the legal restrictions which had been imposed on the police by Leopold II, Pergen expressed desperation at his lack of power to detain men against whom no crimes could be proved in a court of law. Despite Pergen's repeated and urgent requests for this power, however, Francis refused to grant it to him.[42]

It did not take Pergen and Saurau long to fashion an alternative weapon with which to attain their objective. Their chief informer in the ranks of the malcontents, the bookseller Degen, volunteered to act as *agent provocateur*. Degen had little difficulty in leading the men with whom he conversed into speculative talk about how a revolution might be prepared and effected in the lands of the Habsburg monarchy. And when some beer had been consumed, a simple leading question would produce a veritable torrent of incriminating phrases. Degen was always careful to have a third person present at these meetings, who would act as the second witness to the crime required by the law.[43]

In July 1794 a number of arrests were made on the basis of the evidence procured by Degen. The subsequent interrogations revealed something of the extent of political disaffection among the intelligentsia in Austria and Hungary and led to numerous further arrests. Francis was so appalled by the state of affairs as he now saw it that he was prepared to approve Saurau's proposal to set up an extraordinary tribunal for the trial of the suspects, with the power to impose the death penalty, and approved an instruction to this effect to the Supreme Judiciary. The instruction to set up the tribunal came into the hands of the former professor of natural law at the University of Vienna, Martini, who also held the office of Second President of the Supreme Judiciary and who was at the time deputizing for the President during his absence. Using arguments based on the doctrine of natural law, Martini convinced Francis that it was his inescapable duty to grant the accused trial by the normal legal procedure, even if this were to delay or restrict the imposition of exemplary punishments. Francis thereupon drew back from the criminal course recommended by Saurau, and changed his instruction to the Supreme Judiciary accordingly.[44] Austrian criminal law, as promulgated by Joseph II's Penal Code of 1787, fell far short of fully embodying the legal ideals of the Enlightenment. Nevertheless, the preservation of the principle of trial by the normal legal procedure, in the face of the constant pressure exerted by Pergen and Saurau to turn the Habsburg monarchy into a fully-fledged police state, was an achievement which should not be underrated. The last political achievement of the Austrian Enlightenment, it was all the more remarkable for being attained at a time when the age of reform had already drawn to a close.

It was, however, a limited achievement, which did not basically affect the character of the new era of reaction which had now opened in Austrian history. The long political trials; the execution of nine Austrian and Hungarian 'Jacobins' in 1795; the imprisonment of many more under conditions which some could not survive for long; the subsequent interrogations of all those people whom the accused, in the course of their trials, had named as sharing their own views – all this was enough to frighten the people into silence and outward conformity. The censorship prevented the expression of political dissent in print. The Masonic lodges were harried into dissolution by the police, and soon, at Pergen's insistence, Francis agreed that he would not tolerate their revival.[45] In 1802, when Johann Gottfried Seume passed through Vienna on his famous 'walk to Syracuse', he found that hardly anyone was willing to discuss public affairs with him: 'You can visit public places for months without hearing a single word about politics, so strict is the watch maintained over orthodoxy in both state and church. In all the coffee-houses there reigns such a reverent silence that you might think high mass was being celebrated, when no one dares to breathe. As I am accustomed . . . to speak freely and frankly, acquaintances have warned me several times of the invisible listeners.'[46] Reverent silence in the coffee-houses! That was indeed a transformation! In 1791, it was said, veritable national assemblies were being held in some of the inns and coffee-houses.[47] It seems unlikely that Seume was exaggerating. For by 1801 even Pergen considered that the danger of revolution had passed.[48]

Unfortunately, not even the enforced silence which had prevailed since the Jacobin trials satisfied Francis and his ministers. They wanted to go to the root of the matter and change not only people's outward behaviour, but also the attitudes and thoughts brought to light by the trials. In the opinion of Count Clary, the President of the Supreme Judiciary, there was only one way of effecting such a change: 'Our police safeguards the physical health of the citizens; and I do not think that I am taking excessive liberties if I lay at Your Majesty's feet my most humble proposal that the secret police, this essential pillar of the

116 The severed head of Ignaz von Martinovics, one of the nine Austrian and Hungarian 'Jacobins' who were executed in 1795.

Throne and of our general security, should be instructed to take into its care the spiritual and moral welfare of our citizens too.'

This is precisely the policy which Francis put into effect during the years following the Jacobin trials. At Pergen's suggestion, he established in 1795 a commission to re-organize the entire educational system. A senior councillor of the Ministry of Police was appointed to serve on this commission. And in 1801 he transferred the censorship from the jurisdiction of the Court Chancellery to that of the Ministry of Police. Is it not significant that during this period of reaction the Ministry of Police was given influence over precisely those areas of government from which the Society of Jesus had been removed during the period of reform? Is it not significant that, like their predecessors, the new thought-controllers isolated the Habsburg monarchy from the mainstream of European intellectual and political developments?

The manner in which the Ministry of Police carried out its censorship functions made it the laughing-stock of Europe.[49] More than any other department of government, the censorship helped to create the nineteenth-century image of the Habsburg monarchy as the most anachronistic state in Europe outside Russia. The image was, of course, a superficial one. No amount of reaction and renewed isolation could altogether undo the effects of half a century of radical reform and cultural contacts; and however much they turned their faces against reform, Francis and Metternich could not help but be the beneficiaries of the reforms already carried out.

Under the political surface, where a 'reverent silence' was enforced, the social and cultural development of the people, stimulated by the earlier reforms and the Enlightenment, continued. We can see it in the advance of industry, achieved in the teeth of restrictions prompted by fears of social unrest. We can see it in the Viennese popular comedy, which continued to flourish in the suburban theatres, and through which the successors of Stranitzky, foremost among them Nestroy, reasserted the right of the people to make their comments on what was going on in the world, in defiance of the police censorship. We can see it, above all perhaps, in Austrian music, in which the tradition inaugurated by Mozart in *The Magic Flute* lived on, magnificently developed by Haydn in his great oratorios and by Beethoven. These were the late fruits of the Austrian achievement in the age of Enlightenment, through which it continued its contribution to the heritage of European civilization.

117 'Freedom is very dear to us, and living in slavery is not. Therefore . . . we are 197.' One of the many subversive leaflets, indicating widespread political discontent, found by Pergen's police in 1794.

1699	Treaty of Carlowitz signed by Austria, Poland, Venice and Ottoman Empire: Habsburg sovereignty extended to the whole of Hungary.
1701	Austria embarks on the struggle for the Spanish Habsburg inheritance.
1702	Grand Alliance against Louis XIV renewed.
1703	Vienna's first regular newspaper, the *Wienerische Diarium*, launched.
1704	Prince Eugene of Savoy and the Duke of Marlborough defeat the French army at Blenheim (Hochstädt).
1705	Eugene expels French forces from northern Italy. Death of the Holy Roman Emperor, Leopold I. Accession of Joseph I.
1706–9	Eugene's and Marlborough's victories in the Netherlands.
1710	*Kärntnertortheater* in Vienna taken over by Stranitzky's company of German players.
1711	Death of Joseph I. Election of Charles VI as Holy Roman Emperor.
1712	Eugene's mission to London to keep Great Britain in the Grand Alliance.
1713	Great Britain and the United Provinces conclude separate Peace of Utrecht. Pragmatic Sanction.
1714	Treaty of Rastatt signed by Austria, the Empire and France: Austria gains former Spanish possessions in Italy and the Netherlands.
1716–18	Renewed war between Austria and the Ottoman Empire.
1718	Treaty of Passarowitz: Austria gains part of Serbia and Belgrade.
1720	Acquisition of Sicily from Savoy in exchange for Sardinia
1722	Hungarian Diet recognizes the Pragmatic Sanction.
1725	Treaty of Vienna signed by Austria and Spain: Charles VI renounces claim to Spain.
1731	Treaty of Vienna signed by Great Britain, the United Provinces, Spain and Austria: Ostend East India Company suppressed in return for British guarantee of the Pragmatic Sanction.
1733–35	War of the Polish Succession.
1734–35	Austria loses Naples and Sicily to Spain.
1736	Death of Eugene. Marriage of Maria Theresa, daughter of Charles VI, to Francis, Duke of Lorraine, who is compelled to exchange his patrimony for Tuscany.
1737–39	Austro-Turkish War results from the outbreak of the Russo-Turkish War in 1735.
1739	Austria, Russia and the Ottoman Empire sign the Treaty of Belgrade: Austria loses Serbia and Belgrade. Raphael Donner's *Mehlmarktbrunnen*.

1740	Death of Charles VI. Accession of Maria Theresa to sovereignty over the Habsburg dominions. Accession of Frederick II (the Great) as King of Prussia; Prussian troops invade Silesia.
1741	Battle of Mollwitz; Prussian conquest of Silesia. French and Bavarian troops occupy Bohemia and Upper Austria, whose Estates do homage to Charles Albert, Elector of Bavaria, supporting his claim to succeed Charles VI as Holy Roman Emperor. Hungarian Diet calls out the Feudal Levy to support Maria Theresa against Charles Albert.
1742	Charles Albert crowned as Holy Roman Emperor, Charles VII, at Frankfurt-am-Main.
1742–43	Austrian troops reconquer Bohemia and Upper Austria.
1745	Death of Charles Albert. Election of Francis, Duke of Lorraine, as Holy Roman Emperor (Francis I). Treaty of Dresden signed by Austria and Prussia: Austria cedes Silesia. Battle of Fontenoy; French troops occupy Austrian Netherlands.
1748	Treaty of Aix-la-Chapelle ends the War of the Austrian Succession: Austria recovers Netherlands.
1749	Administrative reorganization of the Habsburg monarchy: centralized *Directorium in Publicis et Cameralibus* set up. Beginning of reform of the Austrian universities.
1750–53	Count Kaunitz Austrian ambassador in Paris.
1753	Kaunitz appointed Chancellor of State.
1754	Chair of Natural Law established at the University of Vienna.
1756	Convention of Westminster signed by Great Britain and Prussia: Prussia agrees to ensure the security of Hanover. Treaty of Versailles, signed by Austria and France, ends the Bourbon-Habsburg enmity. Frederick II's invasion of Saxony begins the Seven Years' War.
1757	Prussian invasion of Bohemia; the Battle of Prague. Count Daun's victory at Kolin saves Bohemia for Austria.
1759	Russian army defeats Frederick II at Kunersdorf.
1761	Lack of money compels reduction in Austrian army strength. Council of State set up to co-ordinate all internal affairs of the Habsburg monarchy.
1762	Death of the Empress Elizabeth of Russia; Russia withdraws from the war against Prussia.
1763	Treaty of Paris signed by Great Britain, France and Spain. Treaty of Hubertusburg signed by Austria and Prussia: Prussia retains Silesia.
1764	Hungarian Diet refuses to vote a substantial increase in subsidy.
1765	Death of Francis I. His second son, Leopold, succeeds him as Grand Duke of Tuscany. Joseph, son of Francis I and Maria Theresa, elected as Holy Roman Emperor (Joseph II) and appointed co-regent of Habsburg monarchy.
1766	Incorporation of Lorraine in France.
1767	Department of Ecclesiastical Affairs set up in Vienna under Ritter von Heinke. Beginning of regulation of labour services in Habsburg monarchy.
1768–74	Russo-Turkish War.
1769	Austrian occupation of Zips paves the way for the First Partition of Poland.
1769–70	Meetings between Frederick II and Joseph II to discuss the Eastern Question.

1771 First steps towards universal primary education in Habsburg monarchy.

1772 First Partition of Poland: Austria acquires Galicia.

1773 Society of Jesus dissolved by Bull of Pope Clement XIV. Jesuit property in Habsburg monarchy taken over by the state.

1774 Treaty of Kutschuk-Kainardji ends the Russo-Turkish War: Russia acquires the north coast of the Black Sea.

1775 Bohemian peasant revolt. Regulation of labour services in Bohemia.

1776 Abolition of judicial torture in the Austrian penal code. Vienna Court Theatre reorganized as the *Deutsche Nationaltheater*.

1777 Extinction of the Bavarian Wittelsbach Line. Habsburg claim to the succession advanced.

1778–79 War of the Bavarian Succession.

1779 Treaty of Teschen ends the War of the Bavarian Succession: Austria acquires Innviertel.

1780 Joseph II's journey to Russia. Austro-Russian alliance. Death of Maria Theresa. Joseph II becomes sole ruler of the Habsburg monarchy.

1781 Foreign jurisdiction over Austrian ecclesiastical institutions abolished. Patent of Toleration. Relaxation of censorship.

1782 Dissolution of contemplative Orders in the Habsburg monarchy. Pope Pius VI's journey to Vienna. Flood of cheap pamphlets on the religious question. Bohemian peasant heretics transported to Transylvania.

1783 Russian occupation of the Crimea, with Joseph II's diplomatic support.

1784 Treaty of Constantinople signed by Russia and the Ottoman Empire: Crimea and the Kuban ceded to Russia. Alxinger's poem on toleration suppressed by the Austrian censorship.

1784–85 Failure of Joseph II's scheme to exchange the Austrian Netherlands for Bavaria, and to re-open the River Scheldt to trade.

1785 Anti-Habsburg League of German Princes (Fürstenbund) formed. Abolition of the constitutional county-administration of Hungary; Hungary now administered by eight Royal Commissioners.

1786 Joseph II begins to extend his administrative and ecclesiastical reforms to the Netherlands.

1787 Joseph II's penal code published. Riots in the Netherlands against the introduction of reforms. Renewed conflict between Russia and the Ottoman Empire. Joseph II acknowledges *casus foederis*, and prepares to attack the Turks.

1788 Failure of Joseph II's Turkish campaign. Imposition of a 7 per cent war tax.

1789 Growing unrest and opposition in the Austrian Netherlands, Hungary and Tirol. Outbreak of revolution in France. Capture of Belgrade by Baron Laudon. Prussia and Poland threaten to intervene against Austria in the Turkish War. Decree imposing a new general land tax of 12 per cent comes into operation in Austria.

1790 Joseph II revokes most of his Hungarian reforms. Habsburg forces expelled from the Austrian Netherlands by rebel forces. Death of Joseph II. Leopold II elected Holy Roman Emperor. Repeal of Joseph II's land tax decree. Diets convoked in all provinces of the Habsburg monarchy. Convention of Reichenbach: Prussia agrees not to intervene in the Turkish War, and ends her support for the Hungarian rebels.

1790–91 Hungarian Diet: Leopold II's subtle policies help the moderates to prevail over the rebels.

1791 Congress of Sistova: peace terms negotiated between Austria, Russia and the Ottoman Empire on the basis of the *status quo ante*. The Polish Four Years' Diet promulgates a new Polish Constitution. Flight of Louis XVI from Paris. Attempts to organize the intervention of the European powers against the revolutionary government in France. Leopold II and King Frederick William II of Prussia sign the Declaration of Pillnitz, which makes intervention conditional on the concurrence of all the powers. Mozart's *The Magic Flute*.

1792 Austro-Prussian treaty of defence against France. Death of Leopold II. Francis II elected Holy Roman Emperor. France declares war on Austria and Prussia. Resignation of Kaunitz. Brunswick Declaration threatening Paris with destruction if French royal family is harmed. Battle of Valmy, followed by the French invasion of the Austrian Netherlands and the Rhineland.

1793 Second Partition of Poland undertaken by Prussia and Russia, with the exclusion of Austria. Baron Thugut takes over the direction of foreign affairs in Austria. First coalition of European powers against France. Austrian and Prussian troops reoccupy the Netherlands and the Rhineland.

1794 Polish insurrection, led by Kosciuszko, against Prussia and Russia. Battle of Fleurus; the French occupy the Austrian Netherlands for the second time. Arrest and trial of dissidents in Austria and Hungary. Russian occupation of Warsaw ends the Polish insurrection.

1795 Treaty of Basle signed by Prussia and France: northern Germany neutralized. Archduke Charles defends southern Germany against French invasion. Third (and final) Partition of Poland between Russia, Prussia and Austria. Nine Austrian and Hungarian dissidents executed; many others condemned to penal servitude.

1796 French army under Napoleon Bonaparte invades northern Italy. Piedmont compelled to make peace with France.

1797 French army under Bonaparte invades Styria and threatens Vienna. Treaty of Campo Formio signed by Austria and France: Austria recognizes the Rhine as the French frontier and receives Venice at the hands of Bonaparte.

1798 Abortive Congress of Rastatt. Bonaparte's Egyptian campaign. Second Coalition of European powers against France. French forces driven out of northern Italy.

1799 Austro-Russian campaign in northern Italy and Switzerland fails to clinch earlier successes. Russia withdraws from the war against France. Bonaparte overthrows the Directory in the *coup d'état* of 18 Brumaire.

1800 Bonaparte's victory at Marengo enables French forces to reoccupy Italy. General Moreau's victory at Hohenlinden enables French forces to occupy southern Germany.

1801 Treaty of Lunéville signed by Austria and France: French possession of the Rhine frontier confirmed. Secularization of ecclesiastical territories in the Holy Roman Empire, to compensate princes who had lost lands west of the Rhine. Resignation of Thugut. Austrian Ministry of Police takes over the administration of the censorship. Haydn's oratorio *The Seasons* (libretto by Gottfried van Swieten) completed.

ADB   *Allgemeine Deutsche Bibliothek*
AÖG   *Archiv für Österreichische Geschichte*
JG   *Jahrbuch der Grillparzergesellschaft*
MIÖG   *Mitteilungen des Instituts für Österreichische Geschichtsforschung*
VSWG   *Vierteljahrschrift für Sozial- und Wirtschaftsgeschichte*
ZK   *Zeitschrift für Kirchengeschichte*

CHAPTER ONE

1   M. Grunwald, *Samuel Oppenheimer und sein Kreis* (Vienna and Leipzig 1913), pp. 6–10, 68–78, 115–16, 138–43, 150–2

2   H. I. Bidermann, 'Die Wiener Stadtbank', *AÖG*, **20**, 1859, 357–8, 388–9, 400–1

3   F. Tremel, *Wirtschafts- und Sozialgeschichte Österreichs* (Vienna 1969), p. 246

4   I. Erceg, 'Aussenhandel der nordadriatischen Seestädte', *VSWG*, **55**, 1968, 468

5   [I. De Luca,] 'Nachricht von der k.k. Wollenzeug Fabrik in Linz', in A. L. Schlözer, ed., *Briefwechsel*, X (Göttingen 1782), p. 203

6   *Das Merckwürdige Wien*, II (Vienna 1727), p. 74; C. Singer *et al.*, ed., *History of Technology*, IV (Oxford 1957), p. 178, where Fischer von Erlach's name is wrongly given

7   W. L. Wekhrlin, *Denkwürdigkeiten von Wien* (s.l. 1777), p. 9; M. Fuhrmann, *Historische Be-* schreibung . . . von . . . Wien, I (Vienna 1766), p. 294

8   O. Redlich, *Das Werden einer Grossmacht* (2nd ed., Vienna 1942), p. 238

9   W. Kaltenstadler, 'Der österreichische Seehandel über Triest im 18. Jahrhundert', *VSWG*, **55**, 1968, 490–1, corrects the excessively rosy picture painted by H. von Srbik, 'Adriapolitik unter Kaiser Leopold I.', *MIÖG*, Ergänzungsband **II**, 1929, 639

10   W. Kaltenstadler, *loc. cit.*, pp. 498–500

11   W. Buchowiecki, *Der Barockbau der ehemaligen Hofbibliothek in Wien* (Vienna 1957), pp. 87–123

12   *Ibid.*, pp. 85–6

13   H. Sedlmayr, 'Die politische Bedeutung des deutschen Barock', *Gesamtdeutsche Vergangenheit: Festgabe für Heinrich R. von Srbik* (Munich 1938), pp. 133–4

14 *Entwurff einer historischen Archi-tektur*, text by G. Heraeus (Vienna 1721); cf. G. Kunoth, *Die Historische Architektur Fischers von Erlach* (Düsseldorf 1956)

15 H. Aurenhammer, *Johann Bern-hard Fischer von Erlach* (Vienna 1957), pp. 28–43. For Leibniz's idea of a partnership between creative men and God, see his *Principes de la Nature et de la Grâce fondés en Raison*, ed. A. Robinet (Paris 1954), pp. 55–7

16 E. Egg, 'Paul Troger – Leben und Werk', *Paul Troger und die österreichische Barockkunst* (Catalogue of the exhibition in Altenburg, 1963; Vienna 1963), pp. 48–9

17 K. Gutkas, 'Österreich zur Zeit Jakob Prandtauers', *Jakob Prand-tauer und sein Kunstkreis* (Cata-logue of the exhibition in Melk, 1960; Vienna 1960), p. 19. H. Hantsch, *Jakob Prandtauer* (Vienna 1926), p. 81, gives 30,000 florins as the annual sum spent on the new buildings at Melk

18 F. von Mensi, *Die Finanzen Österreichs von 1701 bis 1740* (Vienna 1890), pp. 17–29

19 R. J. Kerner, *Bohemia in the Eighteenth Century* (New York 1932), p. 24

20 G. Grüll, *Bauer, Herr und Landes-fürst* (Linz 1963), pp. 46–9

21 G. Schweighofer, 'Paul Trogers Leben und seine Beziehungen zum Stifte Altenburg', *Paul Troger und die österreichische Barockkunst* (Catalogue of the exhibition in Altenburg, 1963; Vienna 1963), p. 74

22 O. Redlich, *op. cit.*, pp. 148–217, gives a good analysis of the Hungarian rebellion

23 A. Fischel, *Studien zur öster-reichischen Reichsgeschichte* (Vienna 1906), especially pp. 211–30, 263–80, 288–93

24 *New Cambridge Modern History*, V (Cambridge 1961), p. 480

25 R. Halsband, ed., *The Complete Letters of Lady Mary Wortley Montagu*, I (Oxford 1965), p. 280

26 A. F. Přibram, ed., *Urkunden und Akten zur Geschichte der Juden in Wien* (Vienna 1918), 1. Abt., I, No. 115, pp. 197–223; No. 118, pp. 257–61

27 *Ibid.*, p. 209

28 J. B. Kuechelbecker, *Aller-neueste Nachricht vom Römisch-Kayserlichen Hofe* (2nd ed., Hanover 1732), p. 747

29 *Das Merckwürdige Wien, oder Monatliche Unterredungen von verschiedenen daselbst befindlichen Merckwürdigkeiten der Natur und Kunst* (Vienna, January–March 1727)

30 K. Blauensteiner, *Georg Raphael Donner* (Vienna 1947), pp. 33–51

31 *Gedanken über die Nachahmung der griechischen Werke in Malerei und Bildhauerkunst* ('Thoughts on the Imitation of Greek Works in Painting and Sculpture')

32 O. Rommel, *Die Alt-Wiener Volkskomödie* (Vienna 1952), pp. 284–90

33 R. Payer von Thurn, ed., *Wiener Haupt- und Staats-aktionen*, I (Vienna 1908), p. 276

34 R. Halsband, ed., *op. cit.*, I, p. 264

35 Report of the Papal Nuncio, 7 XI, 1665, in *AÖG*, **103**, 791

36 G. Klingenstein, 'Vorstufen der theresianischen Studien-reformen in der Regierungs-zeit Karls VI.', *MIÖG*, **76**, 1968, 343–9

37 *Ibid.*, p. 349; H. Sturmberger, 'Studien zur Geschichte der Aufklärung des 18. Jahr-hunderts in Kremsmünster', *MIÖG*, **53**, 1939, 443–4

CHAPTER TWO

1 See Bartenstein's retrospective summary written in 1762, re-printed by A. von Arneth, 'Johann Christoph Bartenstein und seine Zeit', *AÖG*, **46**, 1871, 146–9

2 P. Muret, *La Prépondérance Anglaise (1715–1763)* (3rd ed., Paris 1949), pp. 205–6

3 Bartenstein's memorandum, A. von Arneth, *op. cit.*, pp. 156–8; P. Muret, *op. cit.*, pp. 426–7

4 A. von Arneth, *op. cit.*, pp. 34–5

5 J. Kallbrunner, ed., *Kaiserin Maria Theresias Politisches Testa-ment* (Vienna 1952), p. 79

6 E. Guglia, *Maria Theresia*, II (Munich 1917), p. 9; F. Walter, *Die Geschichte der österreichischen Zentralverwaltung in der Zeit Maria Theresias* (Vienna 1938), pp. 159 ff

7 R. Khevenhüller-Metsch and H. Schlitter, ed., *Aus der Zeit Maria Theresias. Tagebuch des Fürsten Johann Joseph Kheven-hüller-Metsch, Kaiserlichen Obersthofmeisters 1742–1776* (7 vols, Vienna 1908–25), 1745–9, pp. 469–70

8 F. Walter, *op. cit.*, p. 99

9 From a memorandum of Haug-witz reprinted in A. Beer, 'Die Staatsschulden und die Ord-nung des Staatshaushaltes unter Maria Theresia', *AÖG*, **82**, 1895, 89–90

10 A. Fischel, *Studien zur öster-reichischen Reichsgeschichte* (Vienna 1906), pp. 147, 224

11 R. Khevenhüller-Metsch and H. Schlitter, ed., *op. cit.*, 1745–9, p. 322

12 J. Kallbrunner, *op. cit.*, pp. 67–8

13 *Ibid.*, p. 62

14 E. Guglia, *op. cit.*, II, p. 10

15 *Ibid.*, pp. 35–6

16 J. Kallbrunner, *op. cit.*, p. 71

17 A. Beer, *loc. cit.*, p. 116

18 F. Walter, *op. cit.*, pp. 261–338, 366–421

19 J. Kallbrunner, *op. cit.*, p. 65

20 A. von Arneth, *Geschichte Maria Theresias*, VII (Vienna 1876), pp. 114–16; F. Maass, *Der Josephinismus*, I (Vienna 1951), pp. 40–4

21 A. von Arneth, *Geschichte Maria Theresias*, VII, pp. 129–31

22 F. Maass, *Der Josephinismus*, I, pp. 264–6; *Der Früh-josephinismus* (Vienna 1969), pp. 62–85

23 F. Krones, *Ungarn unter Maria Theresia und Joseph II.* (Graz

1871), pp. 17–18; H. Marczali, *Hungary in the Eighteenth Century* (Cambridge 1910), p. 193

24 Quoted by K. Grünberg, *Franz Anton von Blanc* (Munich and Leipzig 1921), p. 31

25 *Ibid.*, pp. 32–48; E. Murr Link, *The Emancipation of the Austrian Peasant 1740–1798* (New York 1949), pp. 47–61

26 K. Grünberg, *op. cit.*, pp. 48–59; E. Guglia, *op. cit.*, II, pp. 352–6; F. Fejtö, *Un Habsbourg Révolutionnaire – Joseph II* (Paris 1953), pp. 139–40

27 A. Beer, 'Die Zollpolitik und die Schaffung eines einheitlichen Zollgebietes unter Maria Theresia', *MIÖG*, **14**, 1893, 258–78

28 A. L. Schlözer, ed., *Staatsanzeigen*, X, 40 (Göttingen, July 1787), pp. 475–98

29 J. von Weinbrenner, *Patriotische Gedanken und Vorschläge über den gehemmten Ausfuhrhandel* (Vienna 1792), pp. 161–2

30 G. Klingenstein, *Staatsverwaltung und kirchliche Autorität im 18. Jahrhundert* (Vienna 1970), pp. 73–4

31 A. von Arneth, *Geschichte Maria Theresias*, IX (Vienna 1879), pp. 57–70

32 K. Garas, *Franz Anton Maulbertsch* (Budapest 1960), p. 77; F. Maass, *Der Josephinismus*, III (Vienna 1956), pp. 358–61

33 J. Kallbrunner, *op. cit.*, p. 38

34 For the most recent expression of this view see F. Maass, *Der Josephinismus*, I, pp. xx–xxi

35 For this generally neglected episode see R. Khevenhüller-Metsch and H. Schlitter, ed., *op. cit.*, 1756–7, pp. 184–200; R. Reinhardt, 'Zur Kirchenreform in Österreich unter Maria Theresia', *ZK*, **77**, 1966, 105–19

36 F. Maass, *Der Frühjosephinismus*, pp. 56–7

37 *Ibid.*, pp. 82–7; C. Wolfsgruber, *Christoph Anton Kardinal Migazzi* (2nd ed., Ravensburg 1897), pp. 342–5

38 F. Maass, *Der Frühjosephinismus*, p. 76

39 F. Maass, *Der Josephinismus*, I, pp. 288–90, 386

40 *Ibid.*, p. 103; F. Valsecchi, *L'Assolutismo Illuminato in Austria e in Lombardia*, II (Bologna 1934), pp. 180–3; Wittola to Dupac, 14 January 1779, in F. Kenninck, ed., 'Les Idées religieuses en Autriche de 1767 à 1787. Correspondance du Dr Wittola avec le Cte Dupac de Bellegarde', *Revue Internationale de Théologie*, **22**, 1898, 582–3

41 J. A. von Helfert, *Die Gründung der österreichischen Volksschule durch Maria Theresia* (Prague 1860), pp. 119–23

42 L. von Pastor, *Geschichte der Päpste*, XVI/2 (Freiburg 1932), pp. 249–52; F. Maass, *Der Josephinismus*, II (Vienna 1953), pp. 171–2

43 J. A. von Helfert, *op. cit.*, pp. 229–33

44 *Ibid.*, pp. 302–15; A. von Arneth, *Geschichte Maria*

Theresias, IX, pp. 238–42, 248–53

45 For the 'Reform Catholics' in this period see G. Klingenstein, *op. cit.*, pp. 95–120

46 E. Winter, *Der Josefinismus* (2nd ed., Berlin 1962), pp. 74–9; C. Wolfsgruber, *op. cit.*, pp. 310–25; Wittola to Dupac, 7 August 1769, in F. Kenninck, *loc. cit.*, p. 319; W. Müller, *Gerhard van Swieten* (Vienna 1883), p. 99

47 F. Maass, *Der Josephinismus*, III (Vienna 1956), p. 263

48 G. Wolf, 'Die Vertreibung der Juden aus Böhmen im Jahre 1744', *Jahrbuch für Geschichte der Juden*, 1896; S. Dubnow, *Weltgeschichte des jüdischen Volkes*, VII (Berlin 1928), p. 285

49 A. von Arneth, *Maria Theresia und Joseph II. Ihre Correspondenz* (Vienna 1867–8), III, pp. 360–1

50 P. von Mitrofanov, *Joseph II. Seine politische und kulturelle Tätigkeit,* I (Vienna 1910), pp. 95-7

51 Comments on a memorandum by Kaunitz, 1779, in E. Benedikt, *Kaiser Joseph II.* (Vienna 1936), pp. 263–4

52 C. Hock and H.I. Bidermann, *Der österreichische Staatsrath* (Vienna 1879), pp. 598–9

53 R. Rozdolski, *Die grosse Steuer- und Agrarreform Josefs II.* (Warsaw 1961), pp. 39–40. In this paragraph and in the paragraphs that follow, I am greatly indebted to Rozdolski's definitive work

54 *Ibid.*, p. 41

55 *Ibid.*, p. 104

56 *Ibid.*, p. 137

57 For further details see J. Blum, *Noble Landowners and Agriculture in Austria 1815–1848* (Baltimore 1948), pp. 52–4

58 Memorandum of Joseph II, 1765, in A. von Arneth, *Maria Theresia und Joseph II. Ihre Correspondenz*, III (Vienna 1868), p. 352

59 Joseph II to Maria Theresa, 20 July 1777, in *ibid.*, II, p. 152; there is a translation of this letter in C.A. Macartney, *The Habsburg and Hohenzollern Dynasties in the Seventeenth and Eighteenth Centuries* (London 1970), pp. 151–2

60 G. Frank, *Das Toleranzpatent Kaiser Josephs II.* (Vienna 1881); G. Loesche, *Von der Duldung zur Gleichberechtigung* (Vienna 1911), pp. 92–5

61 G. Loesche, *op. cit.*, p. 82

62 See the full documentation in A.F. Přibram, ed., *Urkunden und Akten zur Geschichte der Juden in Wien* (Vienna 1918), 1. Abt., I, No. 205, pp. 440–500.

63 Allgemeines Verwaltungsarchiv, Vienna, *Studienhofkommission*, F. 85, *in genere* 119 ex 1782. The draft is unmistakably in Sonnenfels's handwriting

64 British Museum, Add. MSS., 35.561, p. 4; see also his report of 11 December 1784 in *ibid.*, 35.562, p. 5

65 Even Pope Pius VI acknowledged his devoutness, as is emphasized by B.F. Menzel,

Abt Franz Stephan Rautenstrauch von Břevnov-Braunau (Königstein im Taunus 1969), pp. 24–5   4

66 Journal of Joseph II's journey to Bohemia in 1771, in R. Khevenhüller-Metsch and H. Schlitter, ed., *op. cit.*, 1770–3, pp. 384–5

67 *Ibid.*, p. 384

68 B. F. Menzel, *op. cit.*, pp. 236–8

69 Hofdekret, 21 August 1786, *Dritte Sammlung der k.k. Landesfürstlichen Verordnungen und Gesetze in materiis publico ecclesiasticis* (Prague 1787), pp. 243–5

70 I. A. Fessler, *Dr. Fesslers Rückblicke auf seine siebzig-jährige Pilgerschaft* (Breslau 1824), p. 85

71 C. Wolfsgruber, *op. cit.*, pp. 559–60

CHAPTER THREE

1 See R. Khevenhüller-Metsch and H. Schlitter, ed., *Aus der Zeit Maria Theresias. Tagebuch des Fürsten Johann Joseph Khevenhüller-Metsch, Kaiserlichen Obersthofmeisters 1742–1776* (7 vols, Vienna 1908–25), 1752–5, p. 196

2 A. L. Schlözer, ed., *Briefwechsel*, X, 58 (Göttingen 1782), p. 203; W. Hofmann, 'Die Anfänge der österreichischen Baumwollwarenindustrie in den österreichischen Alpenländern im 18. Jahrhundert', *AÖG*, **110/2**, 1926, 574–80

3 According to De Luca, a thousand workers worked in the Linz woollen goods factory in 1782; see A. L. Schlözer, ed., *op. cit.*, X, 58 (1782), p. 213

4 F. Tremel, *Wirtschafts- und Sozialgeschichte Österreichs* (Vienna 1969), p. 285; H. Hassinger, 'Der Stand der Manufakturen in den deutschen Erbländern der Habsburgermonarchie am Ende des 18. Jahrhunderts', *Die wirtschaftliche Situation in Deutschland und Österreich um die Wende vom 18. zum 19. Jahrhundert*, ed. F. Lüdtke (Stuttgart 1964), p. 174

5 H. Hassinger, 'Der Aussenhandel der Habsburgermonarchie in der zweiten Hälfte des 18. Jahrhunderts', *ibid.*, pp. 82–3

6 A. von Arneth, *Joseph II. und Leopold von Toskana. Ihr Briefwechsel*, II (Vienna 1872), p. 17, letter dated 14 May 1786

7 C. Riesbeck, *Briefe eines reisenden Franzosen über Deutschland* (2nd ed., s.l. 1784), I, p. 176

8 W. L. Wekhrlin, *Denkwürdigkeiten von Wien* (s.l. 1777), p. 3

9 C. Riesbeck, *op. cit.*, pp. 354–6

10 J. Pezzl, *Charakteristik Josephs II.* (Vienna 1790), p. 311

11 Votum Löhrs, A. F. Přibram, ed., *Urkunden und Akten zur Geschichte der Juden in Wien* (Vienna 1918), 1. Abt., I, No. 203, p. 432

12 J. Pezzl, *Skizze von Wien*, III (Vienna 1789), p. 441

13 R. Khevenhüller-Metsch and H. Schlitter, ed., *op. cit.*, 1745–9, p. 198

14 O. Rommel, *Die Alt-Wiener Volkskomödie* (Vienna 1952),

pp. 362–80, p. 387: 'Die Stegreifburleske . . . war reines Spiel gewesen, das nichts sein wollte als Spiel'; see also Philipp Hafner's biting satire, 'Brief eines neuen Komödienschreibers an einen Schauspieler' (1764), in *Gesammelte Werke*, I (Vienna 1914), pp. 1–10

15 P. von Hofmann-Wellenhof, *Michael Denis* (Innsbruck 1881), pp. 302–3

16 Much of the historical discussion of this question was vitiated until very recently by 'völkish' innuendoes as to the 'sound roots' of the comedy and the 'rootlessness' of its critic Sonnenfels, who was descended from a family of Jewish immigrants. Joseph Nadler's *Literaturgeschichte der deutschen Stämme und Landschaften*, III (Regensburg 1931), pp. 343–5, is a typical example of this

17 H. and E. H. Mueller von Asow, ed., *The Collected Correspondence and Papers of Christoph Willibald Gluck* (London 1962); see especially the letters addressed to Klopstock

18 *Ibid.*, pp. 22–3

19 Reprinted in *Wiener Neudrucke*, 7 (Vienna 1884), 10, 12, 16–17

20 A. von Arneth, *Geschichte Maria Theresias*, IX (Vienna 1879), pp. 271–6

21 The records concerning this aspect of Joseph II's activity have been published by R. Payer von Thurn, *Joseph II. als Theaterdirektor* (Vienna 1920)

22 Cf. Lessing's verdict, recorded by J. H. F. Müller, *Abschied von der k.k. Hof- und Nationalschaubühne* (Vienna 1802), p. 132

23 In considering this question it must be remembered that the issue was primarily a political one because of the non-German preferences of the nobility, and not, as Edward J. Dent assumed (*Mozart's Operas*, 2nd ed., Oxford 1947, pp. 83–7), merely a national one

24 E. Schenk, *Mozart* (Vienna 1956), pp. 567–9, 586. The detailed story of this struggle has yet to be written

25 See the entries in his diary in O. E. Deutsch, *Mozart. A Documentary Biography* (London 1965), pp. 274, 362

26 J. B. Kuechelbecker, *Allerneueste Nachricht vom Römisch-Kayserlichen Hofe* (2nd ed., Hanover 1732), pp. 404–12

27 C. Riesbeck, *op. cit.*, I, p. 292; J. Pezzl, *Skizze von Wien*, I (Vienna 1787), p. 89

28 See H. Ottaway, 'The Enlightenment and the Revolution', in *The Pelican History of Music*, ed. A. Robertson and D. Stevens, III (London 1968)

29 In addition to Riesbeck and Pezzl, referred to in note 27, see Georg Forster's letters from Vienna (1784) in H. Hettner, ed., *Forsters Briefwechsel mit Sömmering* (Brunswick 1877)

30 Letter dated 9 February 1790, quoted in K. Geiringer, *Haydn. A Creative Life in Music* (2nd ed., London 1964), pp. 94–5

31 J. Richter, ed., *Die Brieftasche*, 18. Stück (Vienna, 4 December 1783), pp. 69–71

32 C. Riesbeck, *op cit.*, I, p. 195; J. Pezzl, *op. cit.*, I, p. 28, puts the figure at 32,000 florins.

33 See above, pp. 61–2

34 See above, pp. 66–7

35 G. Winner, *Die Klosteraufhebungen in Niederösterreich und Wien* (Vienna 1967), pp. 52–4

36 K.-H. Osterloh, *Joseph von Sonnenfels und die österreichische Reformbewegung im Zeitalter des aufgeklärten Absolutismus* ('Historische Studien', 409, Lübeck and Hamburg 1970), pp. 31–5

37 W. Martens, *Die Botschaft der Tugend* (Stuttgart 1968), p. 141

38 C. Wolfsgruber, *Christoph Anton Kardinal Migazzi* (2nd ed., Ravensburg 1897), p. 339

39 The best account is A. von Arneth, *op. cit.*, IX, pp. 204–14. For a recent account in English see R. A. Kann, *A Study in Austrian Intellectual History* (London 1960), pp. 186–9. There is an up-to-date summary in K.-H. Osterloh, *loc. cit.*, pp. 165–9

40 Wittola to Dupac, 5 February 1783, in F. Kenninck, ed., 'Correspondance du Dr Wittola avec Cte Dupac de Bellegarde', *Revue Internationale de Théologie*, **22**, 1898, 595

41 Report of 2 March 1782, British Museum, Add. MSS., 35.558, fol. 54.

42 K. Strasser, *Die Wiener Presse in der Josephinischen Zeit* (Vienna 1962), pp. 94–9; interesting extracts in *ADB*, **84/2**, 1789, 311 ff

43 *Marokkanische Briefe* (Vienna 1784), p. 241

44 O. Sashegyi, *Zensur und Geistesfreiheit unter Joseph II.* ('Studia Historica Academiae Scientarum Hungariae', 16, Budapest 1958), pp. 130–1: to my knowledge the first attempt at a serious analysis. F. Valvajec, *Der Josephinismus* (2nd ed., Munich 1945) ignores the pamphlet literature in the chapter on politics

45 In the report referred to in note 41

46 There is a good account of the views expressed in the contemporary journal *Wiener Realzeitung* in C. H. O'Brien, 'Ideas of religious toleration at the time of Joseph II', *Transactions of the American Philosophical Society*, New Series, **59**, Pt 7, 1969, 60–2

47 Alxinger to Reinhold (1785), in R. Keil, ed., *Wiener Freunde* (Vienna 1883), pp. 36–7

48 F. Kratter, *Philosophische und Statistische Beobachtungen, vorzüglich die österreichischen Staaten betreffend*, I (rev. ed., Vienna 1789), p. 19

49 Anon., *Wahrscheinlichkeiten* (Vienna 1785), pp. 87, 94–5, 174

50 O. Sashegyi, *op. cit.*, pp. 96–9

51 *Warum wird Kaiser Joseph von seinem Volke nicht geliebt?* (Vienna 1787), here quoted from the reprint in *Josephinische Curiosa*, ed. F. Gräffer (Vienna 1848), pp. 64–5

52 *Was ist von dem Urtheile des Szekely zu halten?* (Vienna 1786); contents summarized in *ADB*, **76/1**, 1787, 92

53 *Charakteristik Josephs II.* (Vienna 1790), p. 170

54 A. L. Schlözer, ed., *Staats-anzeigen*, XII, 45 (Göttingen June 1788), pp. 31–2 ff

55 'Glaubensbekenntnis eines nach Wahrheit ringenden', *Blumauers Sämmtliche Werke*, I (Vienna 1884), p. 17

56 *Ein Wort im Vertrauen über den Türkenkrieg* (Vienna 1788); contents summarized in *ADB*, **93/2**, 1790, 591

57 *ADB*, **93/1**, 1790, 165–6; the reviewer was evidently misled by the deceptively loyalist subtitle

58 See E. Wangermann, 'Nulla Salus Bello', *Literatur und Kritik*, **5**, 1966, 48–52

59 The superficial works of F. X. Neupauer on Church-State relations are the best example

60 H. J. Watteroth, *Fortsetzung der Betrachtungen über die sittliche Vortheile der Vermischung der Religionspartheyen* (Vienna 1781), pp. 95–6

61 E. Wangermann, *From Joseph II to the Jacobin Trials* (2nd ed., Oxford 1969), pp. 21–3

62 For Riedel's constitutional proposals see A. Körner, *Andreas Riedel* (Cologne 1969), pp. 54–72; for Johann Friedel's views on the participation of the diets, see G. Gugitz, 'Johann Friedel', *JG*, **15**, 1905, 241

63 *Op. cit.*, pp. 29–30

64 *JG*, **15**, 1905, 248

65 See the review of Franz Kratter's *Briefe über den itzigen Zustand in Galizien* in *ADB*, **79/2**, 1788, 591–9, especially 598

66 Carl Ignaz Geiger, *Reise eines Erdbewohners in den Mars*, a facsimile of the edition of 1790 (Stuttgart 1967), pp. 64, 82–3. I am very grateful to Dr Jost Hermand for drawing my attention to this work, to which he has written an illuminating introduction

67 Cf. the anonymous *Die Kriegssteuer* (Vienna 1789), Act I, Scene 10, p. 32

68 Van Swieten to Kaunitz, 16 February 1774, in J. A. von Helfert, *Die Gründung der österreichischen Volksschule durch Maria Theresia* (Prague 1860), p. 287

69 For Weishaupt and the Illuminati see H. Grassl, *Aufbruch zur Romantik* (Munich 1968), especially pp. 211–18

70 Leopold Mozart to his wife, 18 September 1773, in E. Anderson, ed., *The Letters of Mozart and his Family*, I (2nd ed., London 1966), p. 246. The text of *Thamos, König in Ägypten* is in W. A. Mozart, *Neue Ausgabe sämtlicher Werke*, II/6/1 (Kassel 1956)

71 Mozart to his father, 26 September 1781, in E. Anderson, *op. cit.*, II, p. 770

72 On the significance of *The Magic Flute* see K. Lamprecht, *Deutsche Geschichte*, VIII/2 (Berlin 1921), pp. 659–61,

where it is described as the 'apotheosis of the Enlightenment'; E. Komorzynski, *Emanuel Schikaneder* (Vienna 1951); C. Thomson, 'Mozart and Freemasonry', *Marxism Today* (June 1963); P. Nettl, *Mozart und die königliche Kunst* (Berlin 1932); E. M. Batley, *A Preface to the Magic Flute* (London 1969)

73 Mozart to his wife, 7 July 1791, in E. Anderson, *op. cit.*, II, p. 964

74 Eva König to Lessing, Vienna, 11 May 1774, in K. Lachmann, ed., *G. E. Lessings sämtliche Schriften*, 3rd ed., XXI (Leipzig 1907), p. 26

75 *Dramaturgische Fragmente*, reprinted in O. E. Deutsch, ed., *op. cit.*, p. 209

76 Mozart to his wife, 7/8 October 1791, in E. Anderson, *op. cit.*, II, p. 967

CHAPTER FOUR

1 R. Kink, *Geschichte der kaiserlichen Universität zu Wien* (Vienna 1854), I, pp. 297–300; II, p. 601

2 Handbillet, 9 February 1790, in G. Wolf, *Josefina* (Vienna 1890), pp. 111–12

3 O. Sashegyi, *Zensur und Geistesfreiheit unter Joseph II.* ('Studia Historica Academiae Scientarum Hungariae', 16, Budapest 1958), pp. 191–3

4 Quoted in *ibid.*, p. 136; for the general point, see *ibid.*, pp. 129–31

5 Joseph II to Trautmannsdorff, 8 December 1787, in H.

Schlitter, ed., *Die Korrespondenz Josephs II. mit seinem bevollmächtigten Minister in den Niederlanden Grafen von Trautmannsdorff* (Vienna 1902), p. 30

6 O. Sashegyi, *op. cit.*, pp. 137–8

7 *Ibid.*, pp. 131–2

8 *Ibid.*, pp. 123–5; E. Wangermann, *From Joseph II to the Jacobin Trials* (2nd ed., Oxford 1969), pp. 40–5. These two accounts supplement each other: Sashegyi was not aware of all the aspects of Wucherer's prosecution, while van Swieten's contribution to the wording of the Censorship Patent had escaped me

9 O. Sashegyi, *op. cit.*, pp. 138–51

10 E. Wangermann, *op. cit.*, pp. 47–8

11 *Ibid.*, pp. 46–7

12 *Ibid.*, pp. 47–8

13 F. Walter, 'Die Organisierung der staatlichen Polizei unter Kaiser Joseph II.', *Mitteilungen des Vereines für Geschichte der Stadt Wien*, **7**, 1927, 27–39

14 E. Wangermann, *op. cit.*, p. 37

15 *Ibid.*, pp. 36–43

16 J. Pezzl, *Skizze von Wien*, II (Vienna 1789), pp. 200–4; VI (Vienna 1790), p. 936

17 E. Wangermann, *op. cit.*, p. 54. The sweeping resolution of 28 January 1790 is reprinted in C. A. Macartney, *The Habsburg and Hohenzollern Dynasties in the Seventeenth and Eighteenth Centuries* (London 1970), pp. 139–40

18 Allgemeines Verwaltungsarchiv, Vienna, *Pergen Akten*,

X/A3, H83

19 Ibid., H8
20 Note Pergens, 13 January 1790
    (copy), Haus-, Hof- und Staats-
    archiv, Vienna, Staatskanzlei,
    Noten von der Polizei, F. 29
21 Note Kaunitz, 17 May 1790
    (draft), Haus-, Hof- und Staats-
    archiv, Vienna, Staatskanzlei,
    Vorträge, F. 220. It is not certain
    whether a final version of this
    note was submitted to Leopold
22 E. Wangermann, op. cit., pp.
    58–65
23 A. Wandruszka, Leopold II., II
    (Vienna 1964–5), pp. 243–6
24 E. Wangermann, op. cit., pp.
    72, 86; A. Wandruszka, op. cit.,
    II, p. 283. For Leopold's views
    on the importance of govern-
    ment-sponsored propaganda
    see H. B. Jaup and A. F. W.
    Crome, ed., Journal für Staats-
    kunde und Politik, I, 4 (Frankfurt
    am Main 1792), p. 625
25 Allgemeine   Literaturzeitung,
    Intelligenzblatt, 113, 8 Sep-
    tember 1790, 934
26 E. Wangermann, op. cit., p. 91;
    A. Wandruszka, op. cit., II, pp.
    335–7
27 E. Wangermann, op. cit., pp.
    91–100; K.-H. Osterloh, Joseph
    von Sonnenfels und die öster-
    reichische Reformbewegung im
    Zeitalter des aufgeklärten Absolu-
    tismus, 'Historische Studien',
    409 (Lübeck and Hamburg
    1970), pp. 149–57
28 E. Wangermann, op. cit., p. 89
29 Burke to John King, 2 Novem-
    ber 1791, in J. A. Woods, ed.,
    The Correspondence of Edmund

Burke, IX/2 (Cambridge 1970),
p. 439
30 E. Wangermann, op. cit., p. 74
31 D. Silagi, Ungarn und der geheime
    Mitarbeiterkreis Kaiser Leopolds
    II. (Munich 1961), pp. 68–83.
    The printed version of the
    petition of the boroughs
    appeared in A. L. Schlözer, ed.,
    Staatsanzeigen, XVI, 61 (Göt-
    tingen, April 1791), pp. 62–7
32 E. Wangermann, op. cit., p. 107
33 Ibid., pp. 84–5
34 Hofkammerarchiv,   Vienna,
    Geistliche Domänen, F. Rot 2, 22
    ex November 1791, especially
    Leopold's resolution to Vortrag
    Degelmanns, 6 October 1791
35 E. Wangermann, op. cit., p. 85
36 Ibid., pp. 109–11
37 K. O. von Aretin, Heiliges
    Römisches Reich 1776–1806, I
    (Wiesbaden 1967), pp. 262–7
38 E. Wangermann, op. cit., pp.
    114–15
39 Ibid., pp. 116–18
40 Quoted in ibid., pp. 73–5, 119–
    21
41 Ibid., pp. 121–6
42 Ibid., pp. 150–2
43 Ibid., pp. 153–6
44 Ibid., pp. 157–65, 194–201
45 Ibid., p. 175; Allgemeines Ver-
    waltungsarchiv, Vienna, Pergen
    Akten, XA/1, H8
46 Spaziergang nach Syrakus im
    Jahre 1802; reprinted in Prosa-
    schriften (Cologne 1962), p. 196
47 E. Wangermann, op. cit., p. 74
48 Ibid., pp. 190–1
49 Cf. H. Oberhummer, Die
    Wiener Polizei (Vienna 1938),
    pp. 176–93

SOURCES AND BIBLIOGRAPHY

I PRIMARY MANUSCRIPT SOURCES

Allgemeines Verwaltungsarchiv, Vienna: *Studienhofkommissionsakten*, F. 85.
Pergen Akten, X/A1, X/A3.

Haus-, Hof- und Staatsarchiv, Vienna: *Staatskanzlei, Noten von der Polizei*,
F. 29.

Hofkammerarchiv, Vienna: *Geistliche Domänen*, F. Rot 2.

British Museum, London: *Letterbooks of Sir R. Murray Keith*, Add. MSS.
35.551–35.567.

II PRIMARY PRINTED SOURCES

DOCUMENTARY COLLECTIONS

Deutsch, O. E., ed., *Mozart. A Documentary Biography* (London 1965).

Maass, F., *Der Josephinismus*, I–III, *Fontes Rerum Austriacarum*, II/71–73
(Vienna 1951–6).

Macartney, C. A., *The Habsburg and Hohenzollern Dynasties in the Seventeenth and Eighteenth Centuries* ('Documentary History of Western Civilization', London 1970).

Přibram, A. F., ed., *Urkunden und Akten zur Geschichte der Juden in Wien*,
I. Abt., *Quellen und Forschungen zur Geschichte der Juden in Deutsch-Österreich*, VIII (Vienna 1918).

LETTERS AND MEMOIRS

Anderson, E., ed., *The Letters of Mozart and his Family* (2nd ed., 2 vols,
London 1966).

Arneth, A. von, ed., *Maria Theresia und Joseph II. Ihre Correspondenz* (3 vols,
Vienna 1868).

Joseph II. und Leopold von Toskana. Ihr Briefwechsel von 1781 bis 1790 (2
vols, Vienna 1872).

Fessler, I. A., *Dr Fesslers Rückblicke auf seine siebzig-jährige Pilgerschaft*
(Breslau 1824).

Halsband, R., ed., *The Complete Letters of Lady Mary Wortley Montagu*, I
(Oxford 1965).

Hettner, H., ed., *Georg Forsters Briefwechsel mit S. Th. Sömmering* (Brunswick
1877).

Kallbrunner, J., ed., *Kaiserin Maria Theresias Politisches Testament* (Vienna

1952).

Keil, R., ed., *Wiener Freunde 1784–1808* (Letters of Born, Alxinger, Leon and Haschka to K. L. Reinhold, Vienna 1883).

Kenninck, F., 'Les Idées religieuses en Autriche de 1767 à 1787. Correspondance du Dr Wittola avec le Comte Dupac de Bellegarde', *Revue Internationale de Théologie*, **22**, 1898, 308–35, 573–601.

Khevenhüller-Metsch, R., and H. Schlitter, ed., *Aus der Zeit Maria Theresias. Tagebuch des Fürsten Johann Joseph Khevenhüller-Metsch, Kaiserlichen Obersthofmeisters 1742–1776* (7 vols, Vienna 1908–25).

Lachmann, K., ed., *Briefe an Lessing. G. E. Lessings sämtliche Schriften* (3rd ed., XIX, XX, XXI, Leipzig 1904–7).

Mueller von Asow, H. and E. H., ed., *The Collected Correspondence and Papers of Christoph Willibald Gluck* (London 1962).

Müller, J. H. F., *Abschied von der k.k. Hofschaubühne* (Vienna 1802).

Payer von Thurn, R., ed., *Joseph II. als Theaterdirektor* (Vienna 1920).

Robbins Landon, H., and D. Bartha, ed., *Joseph Haydn. Gesammelte Briefe und Aufzeichnungen* (Kassel 1965).

Schlitter, H., ed., *Die Korrespondenz Josephs II. mit seinem bevollmächtigten Minister in den Niederlanden Grafen v. Trautmannsdorff* (Vienna 1902).

Werner, R. M., *Aus dem Josephinischen Wien. Geblers und Nicolais Briefwechsel während der Jahre 1771–1786* (Berlin 1888).

Woods, J. A., and A. Cobban, ed., *The Correspondence of Edmund Burke* (VI, IX/2, Cambridge 1967, 1970).

PERIODICAL LITERATURE

Allgemeine Deutsche Bibliothek, ed. F. Nicolai (Berlin, 1765 ff).

Allgemeine Literaturzeitung (Jena, 1785 ff).

Briefe über die Wienerische Schaubühne, ed. J. v. Sonnenfels (Vienna, 1768–9), reprinted in *Wiener Neudrucke*, 7 (Vienna 1884).

Die Brieftasche, ed. J. Richter (Vienna 1783).

Briefwechsel, ed. A. L. Schlözer (Göttingen 1772–82).

Der Mann Ohne Vorurteil, ed. J. v. Sonnenfels (Vienna 1765–7).

Das Merckwürdige Wien, oder Monatliche Unterrechungen von verschiedenen daselbst befindlichen Merckwürdigkeiten der Natur und Kunst (Vienna 1727).

Staatsanzeigen, ed. A. L. Schlözer (Göttingen 1782–94).

CONTEMPORARY POLITICAL AND OTHER LITERATURE

Alxinger, J. B. von, *Alxingers Sämtliche Gedichte* (Leipzig 1784).

Anon. *Briefe über den gegenwärtigen Zustand der Literatur und des Buchhandels in Österreich* (s.l. 1788).

Die Kriegssteuer (Vienna 1789).

Wahrscheinlichkeiten (Vienna 1785).

Blumauer, A., *Sämmtliche Werke und handschriftlicher Nachlass* (4 vols, Vienna 1884).

De Luca, I., *Wiens gegenwärtiger Zustand unter Josephs Regierung* (Vienna 1787).

Fuhrmann, M., *Historische Beschreibung . . . von der Römisch Kaiserlichen und Königlichen Residenzstadt Wien* (3 vols, Vienna 1766, 1767).

Geiger, C. I., *Reise eines Erdbewohners in den Mars*, a facsimile, ed. J. Hermand, of the edition of 1790 (Stuttgart 1967).

Hafner, P., *Sämmtliche Werke*, 2 vols, *Schriften des Wiener Literarischen Vereins*, XIX, XXI (Vienna 1914, 1915).

Huber, F. X., *Herr Schlendrian, oder Der Richter nach den neuen Kriminalgesetzen* (Vienna 1787).

Kratter, F., *Briefe über den itzigen Zustand von Galizien* (2 vols, Vienna 1786). *Philosophische und Statistische Beobachtungen vorzüglich die österreichischen Staaten betreffend* (rev. ed., Vienna 1789).

Kuechelbecker, J. B., *Allerneueste Nachricht vom Römisch-Kayserlichen Hofe* (2nd ed., Hanover 1732).

Nicolai, F., *Beschreibung einer Reise durch Deutschland und die Schweiz im Jahre 1781*, IV, V (Berlin 1784, 1785).

Pezzl, J., *Marokkanische Briefe* (Vienna 1784). *Skizze von Wien* (6 vols, Vienna 1787 ff). *Charakteristik Josephs II.* (Vienna 1790).

Richter, J., *Warum wird Joseph II. von seinem Volke nicht geliebt?* (Vienna 1787); reprinted in F. Gräffer, ed., *Josephinische Curiosa* (Vienna 1848).

Riesbeck, C., *Briefe eines reisenden Franzosen über Deutschland* (2nd ed., s.l. 1784).

Röder, P., *Reise durch das südliche Deutschland* (Leipzig and Klagenfurt 1789).

Schikaneder, E., *Die Zauberflöte*; complete text in O. Rommel, ed., *Deutsche Literatur in Entwicklungsreihen*, Reihe 8: Barocktradition, 1. Bd: Die Maschinenkomödie (Leipzig 1935).

Seume, J. G., *Spaziergang nach Syrakus im Jahre 1802*, reprinted in *Prosaschriften* (Cologne 1962).

Steinsberg, F. G. Ritter von, *Der 42 jährige Affe. Ein ganz vermaledeites Märchen* (s.l. 1784).

Stranitzky, J. A., *Wiener Haupt- und Staatsaktionen*, ed. R. Payer von Thurn, *Schriften des Wiener Literarischen Vereins*, X, XIII (Vienna 1908, 1910).

Watteroth, H. J., *Für Toleranz überhaupt und Bürgerrechte der Protestanten in katholischen Staaten* (Vienna 1781). *Fortsetzung der Betrachtungen über die sittlichen Vorteile der Vermischung der Religionspartheyen* (Vienna 1781).

Weinbrenner, J. von, *Patriotische Gedanken und Vorschläge über den gehemmten Ausfuhr-Handel in den deutschen und hungarischen Provinzen des Erzhauses Österreich* (rev. ed., Vienna 1792).

Wekhrlin, W. L., *Denkwürdigkeiten von Wien* (s.l. 1777).

III SECONDARY SOURCES

Note: Only works from which material was used in the writing of this book are listed below. Works recommended for further reading are marked with an asterisk. For a fuller bibliography of secondary works, the reader may refer to E. Zöllner, *Geschichte Österreichs* (Vienna 1961).

Aretin, K. O. von, *Heiliges Römisches Reich* (Wiesbaden 1967).

Arneth, A. von, *Geschichte Maria Theresias* (10 vols, Vienna 1863–79).

'Johann Christoph Bartenstein und seine Zeit', *AÖG*, **46**, 1871.

*Aurenhammer, H., *Johann Bernhard Fischer von Erlach, Österreich Reihe*, 35/37 (Vienna 1957).

Batley, E. M., *A Preface to the Magic Flute* (London 1969).

Beer, A., 'Die Zollpolitik und die Schaffung eines einheitlichen Zollgebietes unter Maria Theresia', *MIÖG*, **14**, 1893.

'Die Staatsschulden und die Ordnung des Staatshaushaltes unter Maria Theresia', *AÖG*, **82**, 1895.

Benedikt, E., *Kaiser Joseph II. 1741–1790* (Vienna 1936).

*Betts, R. R., 'The Habsburg Lands', *New Cambridge Modern History*, V (Cambridge 1961).

Bidermann, H. I., 'Die Wiener Stadtbank', *AÖG*, **20**, 1859.

*Blauensteiner, K., *Georg Raphael Donner* (Vienna 1947).

*Blum, J., *Noble Landowners and Agriculture in Austria, 1815–1848. A Study in the Origins of the Peasant Emancipation of 1848* (Johns Hopkins University Studies in Historical and Political Science, Series LXV, 2, Baltimore 1948).

Buchowiecki, W., *Der Barockbau der ehemaligen Hofbibliothek in Wien, ein Werk Johann Bernhard Fischers von Erlach (Museion*, Neue Folge, Reihe 2, 1. Bd, Vienna 1957).

Dubnow, S., *Weltgeschichte des judischen Volkes*, VII (Berlin 1928).

Egg, E., 'Paul Troger – Leben und Werk', *Paul Troger und die österreichische Barockkunst* (Catalogue of the exhibition in Altenburg, 1963; Vienna 1963).

Erceg, I., 'Aussenhandel der nordadriatischen Seestädte', *VSWG*, **55**, 1968.

*Fischel, A., *Studien zur österreichischen Reichsgeschichte* (Vienna 1906).

Frank, G., *Das Toleranzpatent Kaiser Josephs II.* (Vienna 1881).

Garas, K., *Franz Anton Maulbertsch* (Budapest 1960).

*Geiringer, K., *Haydn. A Creative Life in Music* (2nd ed., London 1964).

Glossy, C., 'Zur Geschichte der Wiener Theaterzensur', *JG*, **7**, 1897.

Grassl, H., *Aufbruch zur Romantik* (Munich 1968).

Grüll, G., *Bauer, Herr und Landesfürst* ('Forschungen zur Geschichte Ober-Österreichs', 8, Linz 1963).

Grünberg, C., *Franz Anton von Blanc* (Leipzig 1921).

Grunwald, M., *Samuel Oppenheimer und sein Kreis* (Vienna and Leipzig 1913).

Gugitz, G., 'Johann Friedel', *JG*, **15**, 1905.

*Guglia, E., *Maria Theresia – ihr Leben und ihre Regierung* (2 vols, Munich 1917).

Gutkas, K., 'Österreich zur Zeit Jakob Prandtauers', *Jakob Prandtauer und sein Kunstkreis* (Catalogue of the exhibition in Melk, 1960; Vienna 1960).

Hantsch, H., *Jakob Prandtauer* (Vienna 1926).

Die Entwicklung Österreich-Ungarns zur Grossmacht ('Geschichte der Führenden Völker', Freiburg im Breisgau 1933).

Hassinger, H., 'Der Stand der Manufakturen in den deutschen Erbländern der Habsburgermonarchie am Ende des 18. Jahrhunderts', 'Der Aussenhandel der Habsburgermonarchie in der zweiten Hälfte des 18. Jahrhunderts', *Die wirtschaftliche Situation in Deutschland und Österreich um die Wende vom 18. zum 19. Jahrhundert*, ed. F. Lüdtke (Stuttgart 1964).

Helfert, J. A. von, *Die Gründung der österreichischen Volksschule durch Maria Theresia* (Prague 1860).

Hock, C., and H. I. Bidermann, *Der österreichische Staatsrat* (Vienna 1879).

Hoffmann, V., 'Die Anfänge der österreichischen Baumwollwarenindustrie in den Alpenländern im 18. Jahrhundert', *AÖG*, **110/2**, 1926.

Hofman-Wellenhof, P. von, *Michael Denis* (Innsbruck 1881).

Kaltenstadler, W., 'Der österreichische Seehandel über Triest im 18. Jahrhundert', *VSWG*, **55**, 1968.

Kann, R. A., *A Study in Austrian Intellectual History. Late Baroque to Romanticism* (London 1960).

Kerner, R. J., *Bohemia in the Eighteenth Century* (New York 1932).

Kink, R., *Geschichte der kaiserlichen Universität zu Wien* (2 vols, Vienna 1854).

Klingenstein, G., 'Vorstufen der theresianischen Studienreformen in der Regierungszeit Karls VI.', *MIÖG*, **76**, 1968.

Staatsverwaltung und kirchliche Autorität im 18. Jahrhundert. Das Problem der Zensur in der theresianischen Reform (Österreich Archiv, Vienna 1970).

*Komorzynski, E., *Emanuel Schikaneder* (Vienna 1951).

Körner, A., *Andreas Riedel* (Cologne University Dissertation, 1969).

Krones, F., *Ungarn unter Maria Theresia und Joseph II.* (Graz 1871).

Lamprecht, K., *Deutsche Geschichte*, VIII/2 (Berlin 1911).

Lhotsky, A., *Österreichische Historiographie* (Österreich Archiv, Vienna 1962).

Loesche, G., *Von der Duldung zur Gleichberechtigung* (Vienna 1911).

*Maass, F., *Der Frühjosephinismus* (Vienna 1969).

Marczali, H., *Hungary in the Eighteenth Century* (Cambridge 1910).

Martens, W., *Die Botschaft der Tugend* (Stuttgart 1968).

Mensi, F., *Die Finanzen Österreichs von 1701 bis 1740* (Vienna 1890).

*Menzel, B. F., *Abt Franz Stephan Rautenstrauch von Břevnov-Braunau* (Königstein in Taunus 1969).

Mikoletzky, H. L., 'Die Anfange der Industrie und der Staatsfinanzen in Österreich im 18. Jahrhundert', *XIIᵉ Congrès International des Sciences Historiques, Rapports*, IV, 1965.

Mitrofanov, P. von, *Joseph II. Seine politische und Kulturelle Tätigkeit*, 2 vols (Vienna 1910).

Müller, W., *Gerhard van Swieten. Biographischer Beitrag zur Geschichte der Aufklärung in Österreich* (Vienna 1883).

Muret, P., *La Prépondérance Anglaise (1715–1763)* ('Peuples et Civilisations', XI, 3rd ed., Paris 1949).

Murr Link, E., *The Emancipation of the Austrian Peasant 1740–1798* (New York 1949).

Nagl, J. W., J. Zeidler and E. Castle, *Deutsch-österreichische Literaturgeschichte*, II (Vienna 1914).

Nettl, P., *Mozart und die königliche Kunst* (Berlin 1932).

*O'Brien, C. H., 'Ideas of religious toleration at the time of Joseph II', *Transactions of the American Philosophical Society*, New series, **59**, Pt 7, 1969.

*Osterloh, K.-H., *Joseph von Sonnenfels und die österreichische Reformbewegung im Zeitalter des aufgeklärten Absolutismus* (*Historische Studien*, 409, Lübeck and Hamburg 1970).

*Ottaway, H., 'The Enlightenment and the Revolution', *The Pelican History of Music*, ed. A. Robertson and D. Stevens, III (London 1968).

Pastor, L. von, *Geschichte der Päpste*, XVI/2 (Freiburg im Breisgau 1932).

*Redlich, O., *Das Werden einer Grossmacht* (2nd ed., Vienna 1942).

Reinhardt, R., 'Zur Kirchenreform in Österreich unter Maria Theresia', *ZK*, **77**, 1966.

Rommel, O., *Die Alt-Wiener Volkskomödie* (Vienna 1952).

*Rozdolski, R., *Die grosse Steuer- und Agrarreform Josefs II.* (Warsaw 1961).

*Sashegyi, O., *Zensur und Geistesfreiheit unter Joseph II.* ('Studia Historica Academiae Scientiarum Hungariae', 16, Budapest 1958).

Schenk, E., *Wolfgang Amadeus Mozart. Eine Biographie* (Vienna 1955).

Schweighofer, G., 'Paul Trogers Leben und seine Beziehungen zum Stifte Altenburg', *Paul Troger und die österreichische Barockkunst* (Catalogue of the exhibition in Altenburg, 1963; Vienna 1963).

Sedlmayr, H., 'Die politische Bedeutung des deutschen Barock', *Gesamtdeutsche Vergangenheit: Festgabe für Heinrich R. von Srbik* (Munich 1938).

*Silagi, D., *Ungarn und der geheime Mitarbeiterkreis Kaiser Leopolds II.* ('Südost Forschungen', 57, Munich 1961).

Srbik, H. von, 'Adriapolitik unter Kaiser Leopold I.', *MIÖG*, Ergänzungsband **11**, 1929.

Strasser, K., *Die wiener Presse in der josephinischen Zeit* (Vienna 1962).

Thomson, C., 'Mozart and Freemasonry', *Marxism Today*, June 1963.

*Tremel, F., *Wirtschafts- und Sozialgeschichte Österreichs* (Vienna 1969).

Valjavec, F., *Der Josephinismus. Zur geistigen Entwicklung Österreichs im 18. und 19. Jahrhundert* (2nd ed., Munich 1945).

★*Die Entstehung der politischen Strömungen in Deutschland 1770–1815* (Vienna 1951).

Valsecchi, F., *L'assolutismo illuminato in Austria e in Lombardia* (2 vols, Bologna 1931–4).

Walter, F., 'Die Organisierung der staatlichen Polizei unter Kaiser Joseph II.', *Mitteilungen des Vereines für Geschichte der Stadt Wien*, **7**, 1927.

Die Geschichte der österreichischen Zentralverwaltung in der Zeit Maria Theresias ('Veröffentlichungen der Kommission für neuere Geschichte Österreichs', 32, Vienna 1938).

Wandruszka, A., *Österreich und Italien im 18. Jahrhundert* (Österreich Archiv, Vienna 1963).

★*Leopold II.* (2 vols, Vienna 1964, 1965).

'Geheimprotestantismus, Josephinismus und Volksliturgie in Österreich', *ZK*, **78**, 1967.

★Wangermann, E., *From Joseph II to the Jacobin Trials* (2nd ed., Oxford 1969).

'Nulla Salus Bello: zu einigen Auswirkungen der Aufklärungsliteratur in Österreich', *Literatur und Kritik*, **5**, 1966.

★Winner, G., *Die Klosteraufhebungen in Niederösterreich und Wien* (Vienna 1967).

★Winter, E., *Der Josefinismus. Die Geschichte des österreichischen Reformkatholizismus* (2nd ed., Berlin 1962).

★*Barock, Absolutismus und Aufklärung in der Donaumonarchie* (Vienna 1971).

Wolf, G., 'Die Vertreibung der Juden aus Böhmen im Jahre 1744', *Jahrbuch für Geschichte der Juden*, 1896.

Josefina (Vienna 1890).

★Wolff, H. M., *Die Weltanschauung der deutschen Aufklärung in geschichtlicher Entwicklung* (Bern 1949).

Wolfsgruber, C., *Christoph Anton Kardinal Migazzi* (2nd ed., Ravensburg 1897).

★Wright, W. E., *Serf, Seigneur and Sovereign. Agrarian Reform in Eighteenth-century Bohemia* (Minneapolis 1966).

LIST OF ILLUSTRATIONS

25 Staircase in the Schloss Mirabell, Salzburg, designed by J. L. von Hildebrandt, 1722.

26 Festival procession on the occasion of the 800 years' jubilee of the Abbey Ranshofen, 1699. Coloured drawing. Oberösterreichisches Landesmuseum. Photo Max Eiersebner.

27 Prague. Engraving by A. Sadeler, early seventeenth century.

28 The expulsion of the Jews from Prague, 1745. Contemporary engraving. Photo Eileen Tweedy.

29 G. R. Donner. Engraving after Paul Troger by J. Schmutzer. Albertina, Vienna.

30 Sculpture of an angel, formerly in the Cathedral of Bratislava, by G. R. Donner. Museum of Fine Arts, Budapest.

31 'Providentia.' Sculpture from the Mehlmarktbrunnen, Vienna, by G. R. Donner. Barockmuseum, Vienna.

32 Design by Giuseppe Galli-Bibiena, 1716, for the opera *Angelica Vincitrice di Alcina*, by J. J. Fux. Engraving by F. A. Dietel. Nationalbibliothek, Vienna, Music Collection.

33 Noble Turk. Coloured drawing for a costume by Antonio Daniele Bertoli. Nationalbibliothek, Vienna.

34 Cavalier in eighteenthth-century dress. Coloured drawing for a costume by Antonio Daniele Bertoli. Osterreichische Nationalbibliothek.

35 Actors preparing for a performance, *c.* 1700. Engraving by P. Decker. Nationalbibliothek, Vienna.

36 J. A. Stranitzky dressed as Hanswurst. Engraving from *Turkischbestraffter Hochmuth*, *c.* 1720.

37 Kremsmünster Abbey. Coloured print by J. Ziegler (1750–1812), after Ferdinand Runk. Albertina, Vienna.

38 St Martin, represented as a hussar. Sculpture by G. R. Donner, Cathedral of Bratislava. Photo courtesy Slovenska Národná Galéria, Bratislava.

39 Maria Theresa represented as King of Hungary. Sculpture in lead by F. X. Messerschmidt, 1766. Barockmuseum, Vienna.

40 Battle at Görlitz, 1757. Engraving by J. C. Czerny. British Museum.

41 Prince Wenzel Anton Kaunitz. Detail from painting by J. Steiner. Photo Archiv für Kunst und Geschichte, Vienna.

42 Farm. Engraving by C. Conti after C. Brand (1722–95). Albertina, Vienna.

43 Peasant women. Etching by C. Brand. Albertina, Vienna.

44 Peasant girl carrying firewood. Hand-tinted print by C. Brand. Nationalbibliothek, Vienna.

45 Tobias Philipp Freiherr von Gebler. Engraving by J. E. Mansfeld (1739–96). Nationalbibliothek, Vienna.

46 Maria Theresa, Francis II and their children. Painting by Martin van Meytens II, 1750. Kunsthistorisches Museum, Vienna. Photo Meyer.

47 The widowed Maria Theresa. Painting by Joseph Ducreux, *c.* 1769. Akademie der bildenden Künste, Vienna. Photo Edeltraut Mandl.

48 Entry of Maria Theresa into Pressburg (now Bratislava), 25 June 1741. Anonymous eighteenth-century Austrian painting. Municipal Gallery, Bratislava. Photo Giraudon.

49 Franz Joseph Ritter von Heinke. Engraving by J. E. Mansfeld (1739–96). Albertina, Vienna.

50 Normalschule, Prague. Engraving by C. Kohl. Albertina, Vienna.

51 Johann Ignaz von Felbiger. Engraving by J. D. Schleuen the Elder after a painting by J. G. Reinitius. Nationalbibliothek, Vienna.

52 Franz Karl Freiherr von Kressl. Engraving by J. E. Mansfeld (1739–96). Nationalbibliothek, Vienna.

53 Gerard van Swieten. Gilt lead bust by F. X. Messerschmidt, 1769. Österreichische Galerie, Vienna, on loan from Vienna University.

54 Franz Stephan Rautenstrauch. Engraving by J. E. Mansfeld, 1775. Albertina, Vienna.

55 Christoph Anton, Cardinal Migazzi, Archbishop of Vienna. ?Engraving by J. Schmutzer. Nationalbibliothek, Vienna.

56 Building designed in 1753 by J.N. Jadot for the university of Vienna. Painting by Bernardo Bellotto, c. 1759. Kunsthistorisches Museum, Vienna. Photo Meyer.

57 Joseph II ploughing the field of farmer Ternka at Slawicowiz, probably on 19 August 1769. Anonymous lithograph, early nineteenth century. Nationalbibliothek, Vienna.

58 Joseph II and his brother Leopold in Rome, 1769. Painting by Pompeo Batoni. Kunsthistorisches Museum, Vienna. Photo Meyer.

59 The Neue Markt, Vienna. Painting by Bernardo Bellotto, c. 1759. Kunsthistorisches Museum, Vienna. Photo Meyer.

60 Mass with orchestral and vocal accompaniment. Engraving by J.E. Mansfeld (1739–96), from *Bildergalerie Katholischer Missbrauche*. Photo Eileen Tweedy.

61 The celebration of the wedding of Charles of Lorraine to the Archduchess Marianne, 1744 Engraving by J.A. Pfeffel. Albertina, Vienna.

62 Textile factory at Oberleidensdorf, Bohemia, 1728. Contemporary engraving. Národni Museum, Prague.

63 Looms in Bohemian mill, 1728. Contemporary engraving. Národni Museum, Prague.

64 Spinning-wheels in Bohemian mill, 1728. Contemporary engraving. Národni Museum, Prague.

65 Decorated chest. Zillertal, Austria, 1774. Österreichisches Museum für Volkskunde, Vienna.

66 Scene in the Brühl, near Mödling, Lower Austria. Coloured engraving by L. Janscha, from a drawing by J. Ziegler, c. 1800. Albertina, Vienna.

67 The Lindenallee in the Augarten, Vienna. Coloured print by J. Ziegler (1750–1812). Albertina, Vienna.

68 'Popular Entertainment.' Etching by F.A. Maulbertsch, 1785. Albertina, Vienna.

69 Seller of etchings. Engraving by J.C. Brand from his *Kaufruf von Wien*, 1775. Nationalbibliothek, Vienna.

70 A performance of Joseph Haydn's opera *L'incontro improvviso* at Esterhaz, 1775. Gouache with heads of ivory. Private collection. Photo Nationalbibliothek, Vienna.

71 Joseph von Sonnenfels. Painting by Johann Baptist Lampi. Akademie der bildenden Künste, Vienna. Photo Nationalbibliothek, Vienna.

72 Johann Thomas Trattner. Engraving by J.E. Mansfeld, 1781, after a painting by J. Hickel, 1770. Nationalbibliothek, Vienna.

73 Johann Michael Denis. Engraving by C. Kohl after C. Caspar. Nationalbibliothek, Vienna.

74 Johanna Sacco. Engraving by C. Kohl. Albertina, Vienna.

75 Christoph Willibald von Gluck. Painting by Joseph-Sifrède Duplessis, 1775. Kunsthistorisches Museum, Vienna.

76 The Michaelerplatz, Vienna. Coloured print by C. Schütz, 1789. Albertina, Vienna.

77 A musical evening at the Malfattis, Vienna. Anonymous painting. Collection von Gleichenstein, Kiechlingsbergen, West Germany.

78 Wolfgang Amadeus Mozart. Unfinished painting by Joseph Lange, probably 1782–83. Mozarteum, Salzburg, Internationale Stiftung.

79 Announcement of the first performance of Mozart's opera *Die Entführung aus dem Serail*, 16 July 1782.

80 Ticket to a concert given by Mozart, c. 1784–85. Mozarteum, Salzburg, Internationale Stiftung.

81 Detail (the Baptism of Christ) from the fresco on the ceiling of the theology lecture room in the room in the old university, Vienna. By Anton Maulbertsch, c. 1766. Photo Peter Cannon-Brookes.

82 The General Hospital, Vienna. Coloured engraving by J. and P. Schaffer. Albertina, Vienna.

83 The Josephinum (Academy of Military Surgery), Vienna. Engraving by C. Schütz. Albertina, Vienna.

84 Title-page of Maria Theresa's Penal Code, 1769. Historisches Museum der Stadt Wien.

85 Illustrations of methods of torture described in the Penal Code, 1769. Popular print. Historisches Museum der Stadt Wien.